D0229780

Lettering in Embroidery

Lettering in Embroidery

Janice Williams

B T Batsford Ltd   London

Frontispiece
**'Earth has not anything to show more
fair': William Wordsworth. Metal
thread work letter E embroidered in
the manner of a mediaeval
illuminated manuscript. Types of gold
include most forms of purl, various
methods of couching, padding and
stringing. The background is a
flannel type of fabric**

First published 1982

© Janice Williams 1982

All rights reserved. No part of this
publication may be reproduced in any
form or by any means without
permission from the Publishers

ISBN 0 7134 3956 4

Filmset in Monophoto Plantin by
Servis Filmsetting Ltd, Manchester

Printed in Great Britain
for the publishers by
The Pitman Press Ltd, Bath

**BT Batsford Ltd
4 Fitzhardinge Street
London W1H 0AH**

Contents

Acknowledgements

No book of this kind nears completion without the unstinting help of others.

I record my thanks for the support of the Milne family, particularly Ruth Milne for correcting and typing my manuscript.

For the people who have so kindly lent me photographs, allowed me to photograph their work or generously given me their time (references are to p. nos): Geraldine Gillett, frontispiece; Sybil Williams, 12; Maureen Pither, 26; Christine Smith-Wildey, 51; Alison Whitehead, 60–62; Eirian Short, 80, 81; Norah Holmes, 115; Jane Lemon and Sarum Group, 70, 83, 98 (top, and bottom left), 99 (top); Jacqueline Haywood, 88; Pamela Warner, 107 (top); Heather Jeans, 107 (top), 109 (right); Pauline Heywood, 88 (bottom); Janet Hastilow, 71 (top).

Judy Barry sent me a large selection of work done by herself and her students, from Manchester Polytechnic, which were a joy, and I wish I could have included them.

Iris Griffiths let me look through her precious nineteenth century magazines to photograph from them: 27, 45, 74, 75; and Nigel Temple let me photograph the illustrations that appear on 28 (top) and 29 from his exciting collection of books.

Katherine Christopher lent me a photograph of the Catherine Jacobson sampler, 46, and Diane Pockett lent me the patchwork bedspread, 67 (also used for the dust cover).

Edith John let me photograph her work, 77, 98 (top left); and also the roll of signatures and lamp made by Liz Belton and Florence Semper, 68 and 102 (top).

Beryl Dean lent me the photograph of the Jubilee Cope (photographed by Millar & Harris) 69, as was the mitre on 98 for the Bishop of Lewes; the Guildford mitre was photographed by Phelps & Marchant Ltd.

My thanks to the Dean and Chapter of Durham, 15; Glasgow School of Art, 34; National Army Museum, 35; J. & P. Coats for NDS leaflet, 36; Royal Scottish Museum and Naomi Tarrant, 41, 43, 44; Editor of Gloucestershire Echo, 35 (bottom); The Dean and Chapter of Gloucester Cathedral, 37; The Dean of Salisbury Cathedral, 70 (bottom), 98 (top and bottom left); Vicar of Northleach Church, 97; Vicar of Frampton-on-Severn and Mrs Sommerville, 100; Fitzwilliam Museum, Cambridge, 42; Bath City Council, 109 (left); Northampton Museum, 107 (bottom), 108; and help from June Swann. Also the Victoria and Albert Museum, Crown Copyright, for the use of 18, 19, 21, 22, 24, 25, 28, 35 (top), 40, 55.

My thanks to Audrey Tucker for allowing me to use her beautiful drawings, 116, 117, and for her encouragement.

To my husband, Colin Squire, for alphabet, 114, and his help with our family when I have been absorbed with this work.

And finally to my mother, May Williams, who lent me these pieces and many more which she has worked over the years: 54, 70 (top), 71 (right), 89, 96 (top left and bottom), 102 (bottom), and to whom this book is dedicated.

I Introduction

'Them hath he filled with wisdom of heart, to work all manner of workmanship, of the engraver, and of the cunning workman, and of the embroiderer, in blue, and in purple, in scarlet, and in fine linen, and of the weaver, even of them that do any workmanship, and of those that devise cunning works.'

Exodus XXXV, 35

With rather doubtful 'wisdom of heart' I embarked on this book. I wrote, drew, photographed, and mentally collected, letterforms. As I worked, I realised that I was travelling and reading for, but not actually doing any, embroidery!

Generally speaking, embroidered letters are rarely practised with the needle. They are prepared in cut paper, with a pencil, a brush, crayons or other accepted methods of design. Unlike the calligrapher, I did not pick up a pen, nor hammer a chisel like the stonemason. I did not make a mark or a dot, a stroke or a dash; because letters have to be designed for embroidery in a cool and calculated way. They do not arrive with a flourish. They are designed with a drawing instrument and executed in yarn. It is difficult to learn the craft of lettering through embroidery, as embroidery adapts to the forms already created by others whose eventual letter shapes depend on the implements they use.

As I studied, I questioned – why letters at all? I decided that I loved them because they are one of the few things left that can appertain to the owner and no one else. We share so much with others in everyday living and in the home, but our names belong to us. This was apparent in the study of the embroidery of the past.

Through the ages, lettering has been used in many ways: marking linen and clothing for practical purposes as well as for decoratively marking household and personal articles; even, sometimes, in an ostentatious way, indicating the status of the person by adding, perhaps, a crown; or by decorative use of initials only, presuming all would know to whom the garment belonged. Phrases also were used, perhaps issuing from an embroidered figure to represent speech, like a comic strip; indicating who an embroidered figure was; giving, perhaps, a date of birth or death or even an address; or commemorating an event such as a marriage or the birth of a baby. So often the lettering referred to a person – the donor, the recipient or the worker. There were also verses and messages of an improving kind.

The framework of techniques has been laid down by many authors to achieve a traditional form of work. With these general rules accepted and assimilated, then is the time to explore these in a new and exciting way. This book makes no attempt to cover all techniques nor to deal thoroughly with those techniques mentioned. The intention is to intersperse them with hints and suggestions for further reference to other books or teachers.

The reader is encouraged to explore the knowledge of drawing as much as possible; to study the technique in its traditional form and to learn all about it before moving on to experimental and creative work.

Do not work in a vacuum; be familiar with the forms of letters (curves and straight lines) as well as letterforms; keep letter forms simple, leaving the slick ideas to the graphic designers; make the embroidery workable in embroidery terms and functional for the idea and purpose, working in the idiom of the moment as suited to the idioms of yarn and cloth.

2 History of Lettering

Japanese characters, formed with a brush, giving thick-thin strokes, reading vertically

When man first began to make permanent records of his ideas he drew pictures. These later became stylized into pictograms; but it was the development of letters representing spoken sounds that allowed the permanent communication of language. Interestingly, the use of pictograms has been revived for communication between people of different languages; for instance, in international airports.

Perhaps cave paintings were the first method of unspoken communication; fine examples can be seen in Lascaux, France. Egyptian tomb decorations show hieroglyphics and there the development from pictures to pictograms can be clearly seen on the chiselled and painted stone surfaces.

Even today, the Chinese and Japanese use pictographic characters, each one of which has a meaning rather than being a phonetic symbol. Originally, characters were formed with a brush and the variation in width of the brush stroke was an important factor in the calligraphic art. Characters were organised in columns, beginning at the right hand edge of the page, although nowadays, under the influence of Western culture, they are often written in rows from left to right. Such alteration in the direction of reading is, of course, not so easy with a phonetic script.

The alphabets known all over the world today developed somewhere around Palestine more than a thousand years before Christ. Many alphabets originated in this area, including the Greek one which preceded the Roman form now used. It is difficult to be specific about factors influencing the development of language and lettering; but there can be no doubt that trade played a great part in the movement of ideas.

The Trajan Column, made in AD 114 in honour of the Emperor Trajan, has beautifully proportioned Roman capitals chiselled in stone. It is considered to be one of the finest examples of early stonework lettering of the Roman alphabet.

Pen versions of the Roman capitals resulted in the development of the uncials and half-uncials which were used in Celtic lettering, exemplified in the Book of Kells. Ornamented capitals are found in mediaeval manuscripts all over Europe, and decorated letters were considered an art form in the Middle Ages.

The Bayeux Tapestry, described the Battle of Hastings in 1066 and probably worked some thirty years later, is the original strip cartoon. It has descriptive lettering and also shows early heraldry, as the combatants have figures worked on their shields. Once again, pictograms are in evidence on the shields. During the Middle Ages fabric coverings for armour had symbols on them which were often embroidered with motifs and were called 'coats of arms'.

The invention of printing radically changed the scene, making the possession of books possible for many more people. The appearance of books was also greatly changed, the use of movable letter-type necessitating uniform spacing, whereas in hand written work the spacing can be individual to various combinations of letters.

Handwriting was later greatly influenced by the style of copperplate

An alphabet styled from the letters on the Trajan column

Adaptations of Celtic letters

engraving and by the advent of the flexible steel pen. The twentieth century saw a further struggle to improve handwriting, pioneers in this field included Marion Richardson with her round-hand version and Tom Gourdie with his italic style, based on the handwriting of the Elizabethan period. Countering this endeavour we now have the ballpoint pen, the typewriter and the telephone, not to mention high postal costs, perhaps making the art of letter writing a thing of the past. Unless an interest in handwriting is encouraged, an appreciation of letter forms is difficult to cultivate.

Over the centuries much of the development of writing and lettering can be attributed to the tools and materials available. Various shaped sticks or brushes were used for early paintings and pictograms on cave walls or inside tombs; chisels for carving stone; quills for writing on paper; styli for wax and gravers for copperplate engraving. The inscribing tool influences the shape and development of the letterform by the way it is held, the width of its working edge, the medium (for example, ink) that leaves the final mark. Also the purpose for which letters are inscribed: for posterity – stone work and tombstones; for a shopping list – ballpoint pen and the back of an envelope.

There are other forms of lettering in use in many parts of the world which are difficult, if not impossible, for people accustomed to the Roman alphabet to

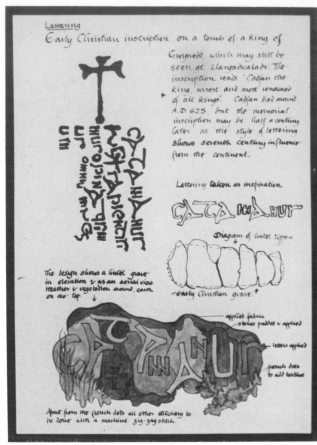

A page from a sketch book and the finished panel using letterforms of an early Christian inscription on a tomb of a king in Wales

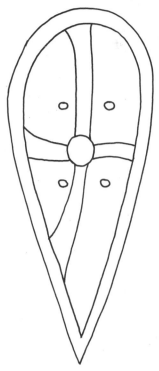

read; these include Hebrew, Greek and Arabic. All lettering, however, has one thing in common – a decorative use. Islamic letter form, for instance, is the sole decoration on hangings and furnishings for religious ceremonies, as the Mohammedans do not use designs incorporating any human or animal shape. Therefore, the 'letter' form is the major part of the design.

Suggested further reading:

Letter-forms and Lettering, John R Biggs, Blandford Press, 1977

The history and Technique of Lettering, Alexander Nesbitt, Dover Publications, 1957

Brief chronological order of development

Fifth century BC	Greek alphabet carved in stone.
Second century BC	Roman alphabet carved in stone.
First century AD	Roman alphabet with serifs carved in stone, Roman edged reed or quill nib.
Fourth century AD	Roman alphabet simplified for speed.
Fifth century AD	Rustic capitals – square edged pen, constant start, nearly vertical nib. Roman uncials, square capitals from written majuscules. For daily use a pointed pen or stylus on papyrus or wax resulting in Roman cursive developing into half-uncials. The quill pen nib was held parallel to the base line.

A diagram showing shields illustrated in the Bayeux tapestry. Were the circular marks secret signs or perhaps carrying strap fixture marks?

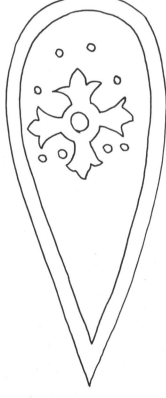

Lettering developed regionally from the fifth century AD in the Holy Roman Empire and those countries who were in contact with it. Missionaries carried it overseas; for instance it is thought that the half-uncial was brought by the Roman Church to Ireland, hence the influence on Anglo-Saxon writing.

From the Roman styles, Charlemagne dictated the use of the Carlovingian writing which developed into what is known as Gothic.

Fifteenth century AD	Moveable type invented.
Seventeenth century AD	Copper engraving reached its greatest technical development.
Eighteenth century AD	The pointed flexible pen was used for handwriting.
Nineteenth century AD **Twentieth century** AD	The Calligrapher and printer diverged.

3 History of Embroidered Letters in Britain

Designers of embroideries have become involved with the craft in many different ways. Through the centuries the lettering has been an addition to the embroidery, emphasising part of the pictorial story, giving information about the embroiderer or the person for whom the work is a gift. The lettering appears to have been designed by the embroiderer or by a designer not solely involved with embroidery. It reflects the style of the time but generally is simple, perhaps even crude. There are exceptions: for example, the lettering on seventeenth/eighteenth century samplers where the designer has considered both materials and the purpose for which the lettering is practised.

One of the most remarkable early sets of work showing lettering is the stole and maniple of St Cuthbert, which is housed in the library of Durham Cathedral. The position of the lettering is vertically placed, but zigzagged. Patricia Wardle, in her *Guide to English Embroidery*, says that the inscriptions show that they were made for Frithestan, Bishop of Winchester from AD 909–931, and the order for them was made by Queen AElffloed who died in 916. It is suggested that it was worked in Winchester. The lettering itself is of Roman-type capitals with serifs, embroidered with coloured silks and silver gilt thread on silk fabric. The subject of the maniple is the hand of the Almighty in the middle, with two saints below and above and half-figures at either end. It is interesting to note that each full-figure saint carries a maniple of similar shape.

The Bayeux Tapestry was worked nearly two hundred years later showing lettering of a similar kind but reading from left to right and usually appearing below the top border. Although the lettering has a similarity to the maniple, it is more developed and of course there is much more of it. The S takes the form recognised today, unlike its S form in the maniple; the E is not of Roman shape and two forms of Roman H (h) are evident. Two or three spacing stops, something like colons, separate most words. The inscription is in Latin. This needlework is preserved in Bayeux; it is approximately 70m (230ft) of embroidered linen, 50cm (20 in) wide, worked in wool inlaid, split, stem and chain stitch. Why, and where, this long panel was embroidered is still a subject of much debate.

The greatest period of embroidery of all time is that referred to as Opus Anglicanum. At no time before nor since has embroidery reached such perfection in design, technique, craftsmanship and liveliness. The English were much envied for their achievements, and gifts of embroidered ecclesiastical vestments were highly prized by recipients in the Church in Europe. There is evidence to suggest that some of the designs for copes, chasubles, palls (and other vestments) and church furnishings were drawn by illustrators of manuscripts. This is true also of the Bayeaux Tapestry, where the stitching is crude but the drawing, particularly of the horses, is masterful. Character, intelligence and many other good human attributes show in the embroidery of the Opus Anglicanum period, which was at its best between 1270 and 1330.

Many of the ecclesiastical garments were decorated with saints and apostles with their names attached, similar to the Cuthbert embroideries. The Salzburg Cope (1290–1310) shows the Tree of Jesse order of design with figures

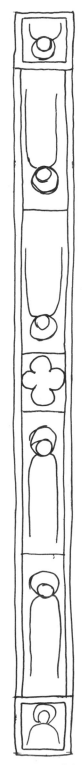

Letter shapes on St Cuthbert's maniple

Position of figures on maniple

The figures of Peter and St John the Baptist on the maniple of St Cuthbert

VVILLELMI

ED WARD

h   e   DVX

The style of lettering found in the Bayeux tapestry

Scene from the Bayeux tapestry showing the position of the lettering

St Thomas' Mitre showing the
martyrdom of St Thomas of
Canterbury dated 1180–1210. This
was worked after the Bayeux
tapestry but before the great period
of Opus Anglicanum

holding a ribbon banner containing their names. This use of lettering is
repeated a number of times in known samples. The embroidery is usually
worked in underside couching in coloured silks with silver gilt thread on linen
background. Donald King suggests, in the catalogue for the 1963 Opus
Anglicanum exhibition in the Victoria and Albert museum, that the frontlet
for an altar is the work of an amateur. It is worked on a white ground, has a row
of gold quatrefoils between two rows of red half-quatrefoils, the former each
containing one letter of an inscription. It is apparently a unique piece of
embroidery as, on the back, in black silk, is the inscription 'DOMINA
JOHANNA BEVERLEY ME FECIT' and is the only known surviving
signed embroidery of that period. Mr King's reason for regarding it as an
amateur piece is that the professionals tended not to sign their work.

The Pienza Cope, so-called because of its resting place, is of the architectural style of design. There are three rows of arches and, in each area
between the arches on the third row, is an apostle holding a scroll on which is
written part of the Creed. An angel holds a scroll with the text GLORIA IN
EXCELSIS DEO, which is a motif repeated in other work of the time. The
delightful way in which each apostle and angel caresses his name, text or
inscribed book, adds to the interest of this and many more superb pieces of
work.

The Vich Cope (1340–1370), which has been badly mutilated in places, has
some very clear lettering, as illustrated. The lettering has a greater degree of
professionalism than many other works from several decades earlier, but the
style of the rest of the embroidery has begun to show weaknesses of the latter,
so-called, Decline period.

The lettering of the Opus Anglicanum period shows the Gothic style of the

Detail from the Jesse Cope worked between 1295 and 1315. This portion shows Jacob holding his name balanced in a delightful way. The figure and branches are placed so that Jacob stands upright when the cope is worn. Note the grain of the background material

Embroidery of Christ enthroned, the work inscribed 'IOHANNIS DE THANETO', who was a monk and chaunter of Canterbury Cathedral. Note the interesting border around his skirt

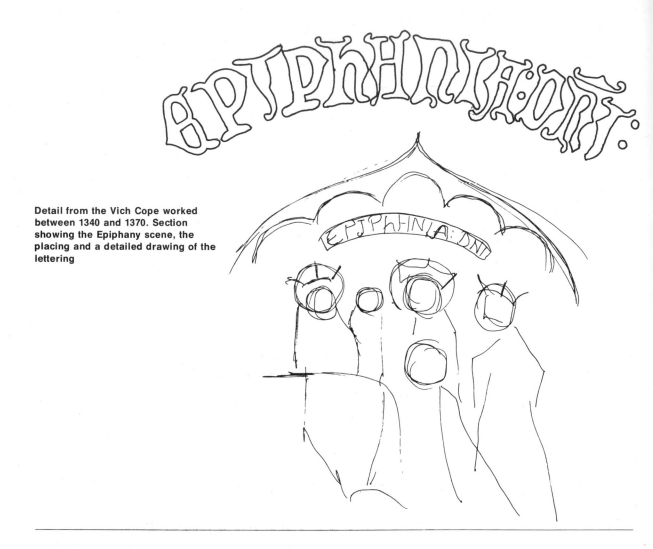

Detail from the Vich Cope worked between 1340 and 1370. Section showing the Epiphany scene, the placing and a detailed drawing of the lettering

The sign over the head of Christ on the Melk Chasuble, worked 1300–1320. Note the spacing stops

thirteenth and fourteenth centuries. This is apparent in some of the Bayeux Tapestry lettering; not particularly well-formed in the mitre of St Thomas, which shows Celtic influence, but very typical in the John of Thanet embroidery. The Vich Cope is of this style and has a flow about it which is very pleasant. The orphrey of a cope (1350–1380) from the church of Harlebeke shows small letters and, once more, the two stops placed like a colon between words.

After the Reformation many fine ecclesiastical vestments in England were taken apart or used for other purposes, and in the event it proved of great value that so many fine articles had been given to other European countries and were thus preserved. It is interesting to speculate on the ways in which embroiderers and designers from monasteries and convents were redeployed

Detail of a coverlet depicting the
story of Tristan in linen fabric with
black linen thread quilting using
darning stitches. It is Sicilian work of
the fourteenth century, showing that
work similar in style to Opus
Anglicanum was being executed in
other parts of the known world. The
letters are placed above the heads of
the figures as in the Bayeux tapestry
and the letterforms are of a celtic
character

after the Reformation; whether the secular embroidery was as grand as the ecclesiastical in the period of Opus Anglicanum; whether, indeed, there was much secular embroidery at all; if so, was it just as glorious as the ecclesiastical but has long since worn out with use; or were the workshops employed only for ecclesiastical embroidery?

At, and after, the Reformation there is much more documentation to accompany work. Portraits show fairly accurate representations of stitchery on costume, for example on the innumerable paintings of Henry VIII and Queen Elizabeth I. There are also inventories telling much about clothes of the Court. Perhaps they were marked with initials or numbers to help record their place in the inventory. In the Bodleian Library there is a book-binding, embroidered by the young Princess Elizabeth as a present for the Queen, Katharine Parr, with the initials KP worked in the interlacing bands.

Mary, Queen of Scots, was a royal lady of great skill with the needle and, of course, she had plenty of time to practise! She shared her interest with her jailer, Bess of Hardwick. There are many panels bearing the initials ES which are in the style of the period of Elizabeth of Hardwick. It is not certain which she, herself, worked. She certainly employed an embroiderer and is recorded as complaining that 'one is not enough'. This household was evidently one where the needle was plied frequently.

George Wingfield Digby says that Nicholas Hilliard, the miniaturist, appeared to be attached to households as broderer. A broderer's business was to cull the many sources of current design and adapt them. Designs came from herbals, flower paintings, natural history books, engravings, woodcuts and also from pattern books. Subjects were often Biblical or mythological.

There is evidence that the panels known as the Oxburgh hangings were copied from books. The 'Shepheard Buss' is partly copied from Paradin's book

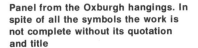

Panel from the Oxburgh hangings. In spite of all the symbols the work is not complete without its quotation and title

One of the medallions of the Oxburgh hangings showing the ES monogram of Elizabeth of Shrewsbury, that is, Bess of Hardwick

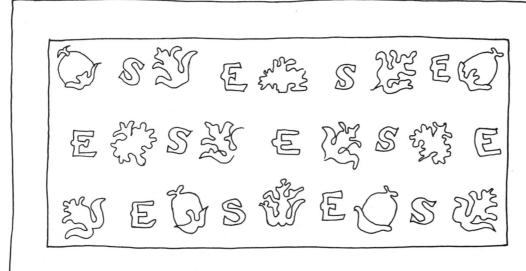

This cushion is in Hardwick Hall, Derbyshire. The letters consist of silk outer cord, inner metal cord and cloth of gold letters. These are applied onto a velvet ground. (Detail of S and part of E)

The Shepheard Buss, embroidered
circa 1600. It is interesting to note the
different way the lettering is used,
from the border rebus to the initials
KB

A handkerchief with a border of meandering honeysuckle in Holbein stitch, an edge of silver gilt bobbin lace and initials EM worked in cross stitch

Mary Hulton's cushion worked during the seventeenth century in tent and cross stitch, showing the Royal Arms of the United Kingdom. It is suggested that this is amateur work because of the addition of the name – presumed to be the worker – in large letters

printed in 1557, as was some of Mary, Queen of Scots' work. The blackwork patterns related particularly well to the block prints of the period. The lettering in the Buss is in capitals, as are the Oxburgh ones; likewise the signature of Mary Hulton on her cushion cover. When comparing all this lettering with the Jane Bostocke sampler of 1596 it suggests that this was the accepted form of embroidered lettering. This sampler has one style but two different methods of working.

Map samplers were worked towards the end of the eighteenth century. They consisted of an outline for the coast, stitched lines to divide the countries into counties, and words, with capital and small letters, broken up to fit into the spaces. Sometimes ships were embroidered in the sea and a scale might be added.

The sampler became well established during the seventeenth century and continues to the present day. It is studied separately in the next section.

Embroidery frequently incorporated names. In the Victoria and Albert museum there is a set of bed curtains and valances from the mid-seventeenth century with the name 'Abigail Pett' embroidered in a rectangle. A work box dated 1692, embroidered with a typical vase of flowers, has the initials PM for Parnell Mackett worked on the vase. Most work boxes of the late seventeenth century were initialled and dated, as were silk pictures.

During the nineteenth century an upsurge of interest was shown in the monogram, the embroidered name, initials, and crown or coronet. This is

A modern map sampler portraying a district of Gloucestershire and the fauna and flora found there

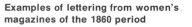
Examples of lettering from women's magazines of the 1860 period

HR in drapes and flowers. [*The Englishwoman's Domestic Magazine*, September 1867]

Elisabeth with lilies and strapwork. [*The Englishwoman's Domestic Magazine*, September 1867]

Initials AL suitable to be embroidered on net and the net inserted into a handkerchief. [*The Queen, The Lady's Newspaper*, 26 November 1870, Supplement]

A butterfly motif with initials LR incorporated into the wings. [*The Englishwoman's Domestic Magazine*, August 1867]

particularly in evidence in ladies' magazines. It was suggested that these were used for handkerchiefs, as well as for underwear and nightwear. They were worked in linen thread on linen or silk thread on silk.

Other embroidered lettering in the nineteenth century includes Victorian card work. These were punched cards worked in cross stitch; often a motto such as 'Home Sweet Home'.

William Morris had a finger in every artistic pie. He added lettering to his embroidery designs with the same confidence that he employed in other fields.

A small concertina folder of alphabets and motifs

Note the date on this collection of motifs and edgings

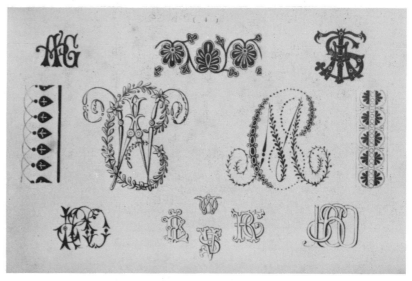

A linen handkerchief trimmed with Valenciennes lace with an embroidered border and monogram of Queen Alexandra to whom the handkerchief belonged as Princess of Wales; worked in the second half of the nineteenth century

He used the mediaeval device of identifying figures by drawing them holding a sash on which their name was inscribed. He also placed the name at the top or the bottom of the work, using capitals, as did other designers working in a similar style.

Other influences around the turn of the century include Jessie Newbery, wife of Francis H Newbery, Director of the Glasgow School of Art. She founded an embroidery class at the School in 1894, developing her own style of embroidery. She was assisted by Ann Macbeth and between them they made lettering an important feature of some of their embroideries. The materials they preferred to use were linen backgrounds with applied silks and linens, and linen and silk yarns. This was a totally different style of work after years of commercial Berlin wool work and they were instrumental in influencing the embroidery of the twentieth century.

Two main sections of the study of lettering in embroidery have so far been omitted but will be mentioned briefly here. These are military lettering, particularly found on pennants, banners and colours. Military regalia is a very specialised and vast subject, the embroidery of which is executed mainly by professional workshops.

Then there are banners. Banners for Boy Scouts, Girls' Brigade, Red Cross, Trade Unions and Mothers' Unions and numerous other organisations. Many

Victorian punchcard embroidery. The words 'WEEDS', 'FLOWERS' and 'SEA' are worked in beads. A delightful little folder tied with ribbons

An example of the preoccupation of
the nineteenth-century designer with
good lettering is shown in this copy
of a title page

2nd edition.

... *The Book of* ...
ORNAMENTAL ALPHABETS

· · ·

Ancient and Modern

*from eighth to nineteenth century, with Numerals
including Gothic; Church text, large and small;
German arabesque; initials for illuminations,
monograms and crosses etc.*

and with

An Analysis of the Roman and Old English Alphabets
(*Large and Small*)

for the use of

**Architectural and Engineering draughtsmen, masons,
decorative painters, lithographers, engravers, carvers,
etc, etc.**

collected and designed by F. Delamotte.

London, E. & F.N. Spon   *1859*

Lettering and design for an orphrey
of a cope. A W N Pugin, *Glossary of
Ecclesiastical Ornament*, 1846

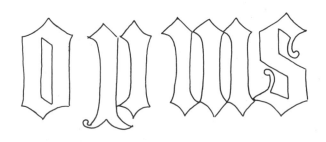

F Delamotte – from his *Ornamental Alphabets Ancient and Modern*, 1846

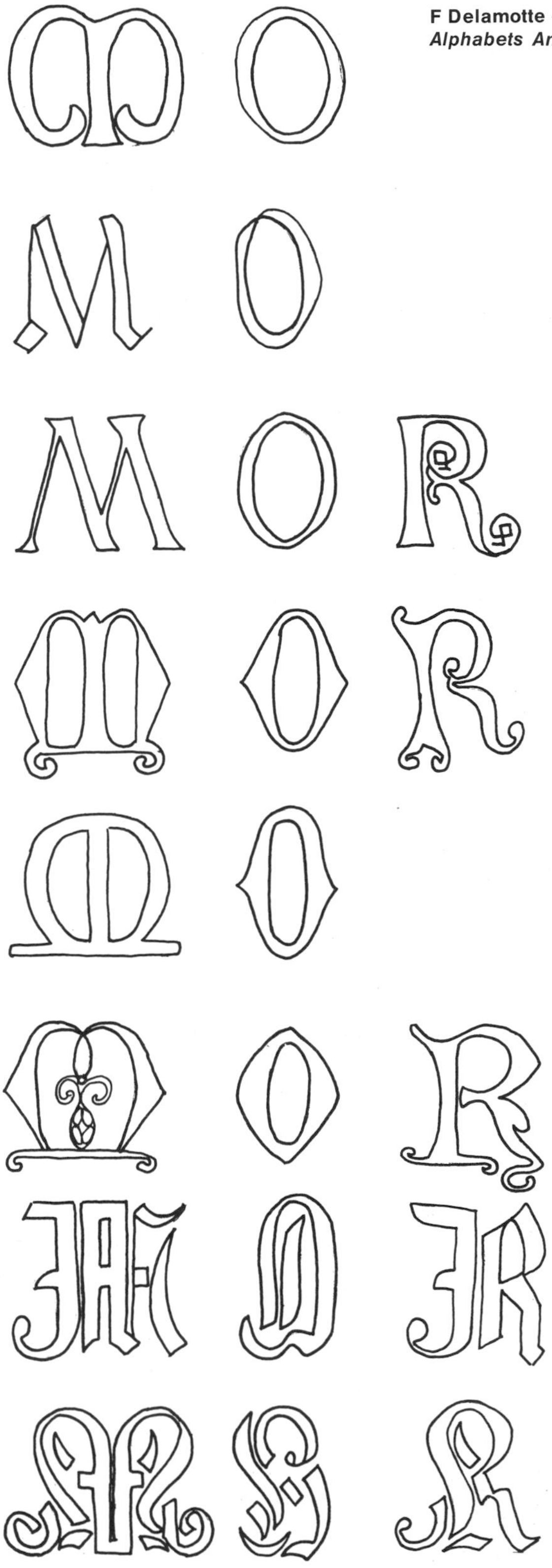

Ninth-century Anglo Saxon

Eighth-century Vatican

**Tenth-century
British Museum**

**Twelfth-century
British Museum**

circa 1340

**Fourteenth-century
British Museum**

Sixteenth-century Gothic ms.

Seventeenth-century ms.

of these are painted, or have motifs and letters of applied bunting onto bunting. Some are very elaborate; there are many ecclesiastical banners displaying intricate metal thread and silk embroidery and great craftsmanship. They date from the end of last century.

During the first half of the twentieth century there were a number of embroiderers who tried to raise embroidery from the crater into which it had fallen. In the late 1950s the Princess Royal, addressing students at the Royal School of Needlework, asked if the twentieth century would be remembered by the copies of embroideries it had made of fine pieces of work of previous centuries! But the Needlework Development Scheme (NDS) was already designing and distributing leaflets to educational establishments and wherever else they were requested. Amongst these leaflets was one on lettering; not particularly exciting but sound in principle (as was much of their work) giving guidance and advice on how to achieve something original and therefore

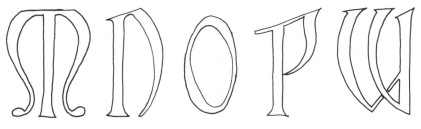

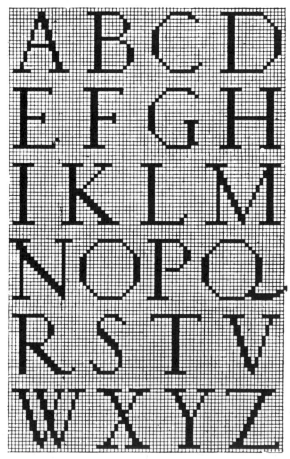

encouraging creativity. (NDS leaflet 28b 'And so to Embroider – Designing with Letters'.) The remarkable point about the NDS leaflet is the reintroduction of lettering in five different forms. So simple, compared to Dillmont, but it fulfils a need created by the loss of tradition, particularly the passing down of methods within families, or the individual education of a few by governesses. In this leaflet initials and lettering are shown placed upon an article and the cross-stitch is illustrated by a photographed sampler, not just indicated by graph paper.

Townswomen's Guilds, Women's Institutes and Local Education Authority evening classes started an upsurge of post war development. Constance Howard's panel depicting Women's Institute members, made for the Festival of Britain in 1951, was an inspiration. The 1960s reflected the times with the lavish use of fabric and thread, but with little use of lettering, except on kneelers in canvas work. New kneelers in churches and cushions in cathedrals began to appear in abundance. Under the capable eyes of experienced needlewomen the less practised and able stitched away in memory of someone, to portray some organisation to which they belonged, or just because they desired to do their bit to liberally distribute around a church a new burst of colour. Lettering was often used to record individual people, societies and associations or special benefactors, and these pieces of work form a great contribution to twentieth century embroidery.

Lewis F Day, from *Alphabets Old and New*, **1899**

Delamotte alphabet from his
Ornamental Alphabets Ancient and
Modern

Design for a pulpit fall in pencil and
watercolour. It is interesting to note
the similarity of the Patten Wilson
alphabet on p. 33 with that used by
Jessie Newbery in her work shown here

Worked about 1865 in wool and silk embroidery in cross stitch with glass and metal beads

A cap of the Royal Regiment of Ireland circa 1710

The parade of the Mothers' Union banners at St Stephen's Church, Cheltenham on 7 May 1958

One example of the cards sent home by soldiers during the First World War, some neatly worked, some crudely and some by machine. French as well as English?

Needlework Development Scheme leaflet

Two choir stall cushions for Gloucester Cathedral depicting the River Severn and its fish, and a decorative way of showing Bishop Hooper's dates

A brief and generalized analysis to date samplers

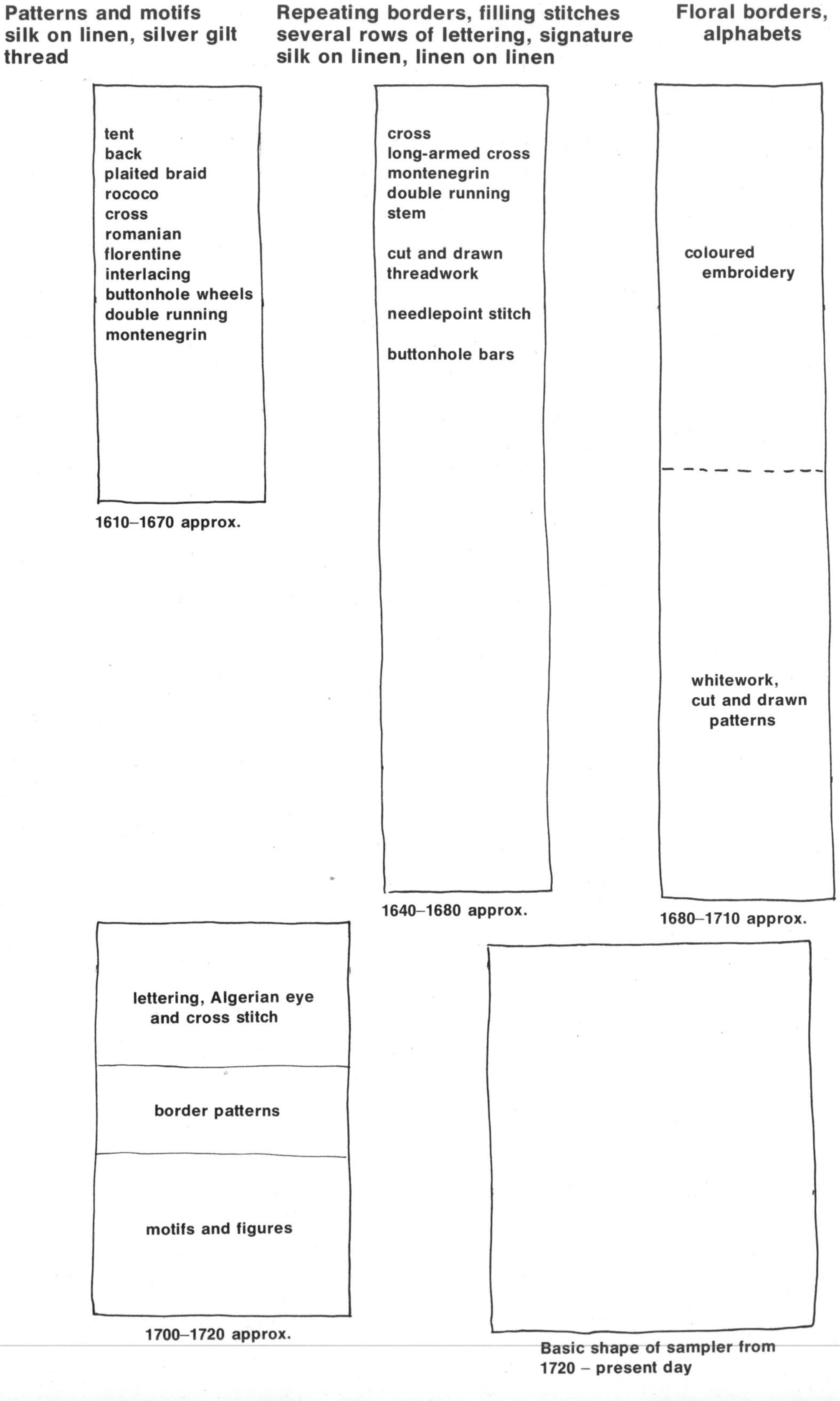

Patterns and motifs silk on linen, silver gilt thread

tent
back
plaited braid
rococo
cross
romanian
florentine
interlacing
buttonhole wheels
double running
montenegrin

1610–1670 approx.

Repeating borders, filling stitches several rows of lettering, signature silk on linen, linen on linen

cross
long-armed cross
montenegrin
double running
stem

cut and drawn
threadwork

needlepoint stitch

buttonhole bars

1640–1680 approx.

Floral borders, alphabets

coloured
embroidery

whitework,
cut and drawn
patterns

1680–1710 approx.

lettering, Algerian eye
and cross stitch

border patterns

motifs and figures

1700–1720 approx.

Basic shape of sampler from
1720 – present day

border patterns

crowns and coronets

figures

name and date
alphabets

1720–1755 approx.

border pattern

motifs including a
home, vases, name and
date

1755–1860 approx.

Berlin wool work scroll, brightly
coloured motifs and patterns

Twentieth century sampler pack
sold to commemorate royal
occasions or for hanging in
the home

Lettering in embroidered samplers

Samplers have been worked consistently for more than three hundred years. There are examples that show experimental work as far back as Egyptian times. In English samplers there was no lettering, except initials and royal insignia, until about 1630. There are exceptions such as the Jane Bostocke sampler of 1598 which records the birth of Alice Lee. The lettering comes below some animals embroidered in a random fashion and below it is a maze of patterns. For two decades samplers were embroidered on linen with silk except where drawn and cut patterns were embroidered with natural coloured linens. This is the general format but with some exceptions. The samplers were narrow and long, restricted by the woven width, until the last part of the eighteenth century, when they became wider and shorter.

Many samplers after 1630 were both named and dated, sometimes recording the age of the worker, the name of the teacher or school and a short quotation. Some also had alphabets. The names and the alphabets were mostly in capital letters, usually reasonably well formed, sometimes repeated should the first row not be satisfactory. Lower case alphabets were also occasionally included. It is delightful to study the sampler of Mary Burrowesis, in the Victoria and Albert Museum, with its inconsistencies.

Capital letters in cut and drawn thread work and needlepoint lace seem more professional; but perhaps the nature of this work has to be more precise and therefore would only be attempted by the able needlewoman.

By 1680 there was evidence of the alphabet having a more important place in the sampler. Examples show up to eight alphabets in one piece. The linen background began to be replaced by a wool canvas.

After 1720 lettering had begun to play a greater part in many of the

A remarkable cut work alphabet worked in the middle or during the second half of the seventeenth century. This is a very professional piece of work

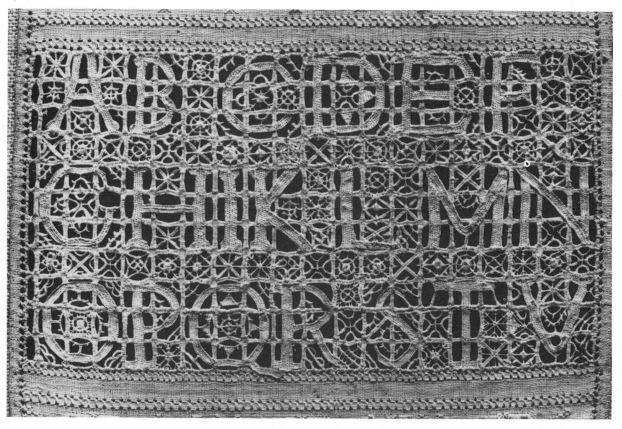

A sampler dated 1734 showing an alphabet and a delightful rendering of the Lord's Prayer, the Ten Commandments and border designs

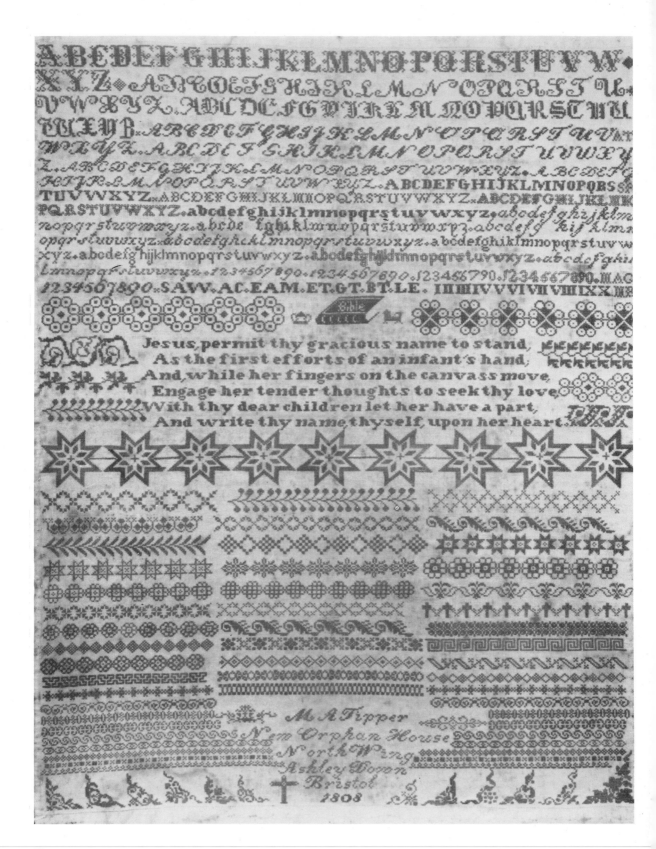

Coloured silk on linen work,
carnation border and alphabets on
the sampler by Margaret Caderhead
in 1812

An amazing collection of alphabets
and borders worked at the New
Orphan Home, Ashley Down, Bristol,
by M A Tipper in 1808

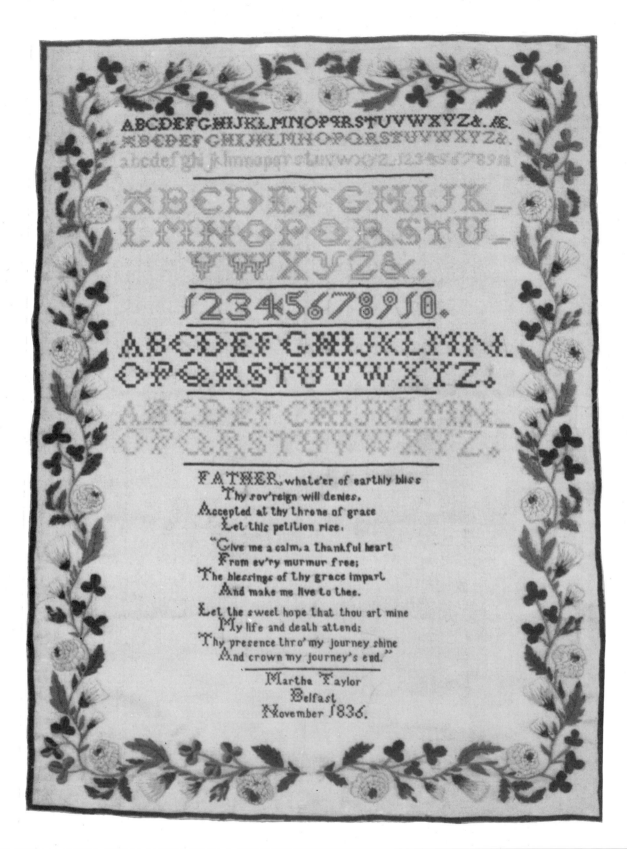

samplers. Psalms, the Lord's Prayer, the Creed and many other religious passages had been diligently practised in thread. Uplifting verses upholding great virtues are found in abundance, stitched with lesser or greater skill, including at least one alphabet, name and a date. Pictorial motif patterns helped fill every corner and by 1750 there was, more often than not, a floral border. The shape was nearly square and often a lower and upper case alphabet was included; numbers and crowns of different kinds also seemed to feature fairly frequently.

Towards the end of the eighteenth century darning patterns appeared. These patterns sometimes filled floral shapes but at other times the patterns created a cross shape of the darning in each direction. There was little lettering; perhaps the name and date only.

Treasures are found from the eighteenth century such as Hannah Haynes' hollie point name in the middle of a hollie point sampler, probably worked in mid-century. Other works of a non-religious kind are the sampler maps and such ideas as a perpetual almanac.

The almost square sampler continued into the nineteenth century, with its pious poems, floral border and house front, gradually degenerating into a cross stitch sampler – charming in its own way but lacking the vitality and colour of the previous decades. The lettering was mostly cross stitch, some Algerian eye and quite carefully worked decorated cross stitch capitals and small letters.

There were other samplers from the middle of the nineteenth century but these were often very long rolls executed in Berlin wool work. By the end of the century the young pupil teacher was spending her time making half-scale

Martha Taylor from Belfast worked this beautifully balanced piece in 1836 with very strong coloured flowers in the border

A design from a magazine of the 1860s showing several styles of alphabets. [*The Englishwoman's Domestic Magazine*, November 1867]

cuffs, apron tops or quarter scale skirts in preparation for her future teaching post. She included a marking cross stitch of some kind; this was part of the technical exercise in preparation for marking linen.

The twentieth century has seen a profusion of transfer samplers, often created to celebrate royal weddings, coronations and jubilees, as well as pictures of a more homely nature. The transfer can be applied to any fabric of the worker's choice and it is often embroidered totally in cross stitch. The colours are selected and dictated by the magazine's designer, so that little but needle plugging is left for the 'embroiderer'. There is no room for any imaginative treatment but, perhaps, this work then reaches a wider public.

Young school children use their own or their friends' initials in many ways (sometimes not in acceptable ways in civilised terms!). But their basic knowledge of lettering and letter form is limited and so, through embroidery, a

The Catherine Jacobson sampler, worked in 1867, shows a similarity in lettering design to the alphabets in the previous photo

I · ONLY · RECORD
THE · SUNNY
HOURS

A commercial sampler of 1951 showing the characteristic crinoline girl

greater appreciation can be cultivated, certainly in the field of the sampler. There are so many ways for young and old to try lettering and embroidery together, and what better way than entwining initials of loved ones or families in various embroidery methods? Metal thread enhancing machine work or quilting or canvas work; French knots on machine embroidery; applied letters on clothing – the combination is unlimited and the experimental trial piece constitutes a sampler.

English Embroidery, AF Kendrick, Batsford, 1913
Guide to English Embroidery, Patricia Wardle, V. & A., 1970

4 Canvas work

Canvas work techniques evolved in several different ways, at different periods of history and in different places. The late mediaeval period produced factory-made wall hangings, woven on enormous looms. Some of the best of these were produced on the Continent of Europe but the cost of the work, shipping charges and the difficulty of communicating with the workers resulted in the development of an imitation work. Thus arose the beginnings of the misinterpretation of the word 'tapestry'. Tapestry is woven on a loom; canvas work entails plying the needle over another, already woven, fabric and is also referred to as needlepoint. Therefore, in England by Tudor times, canvas work was a well established form of needlework carried out in the home by the lady of the house and her maids. It was used for hangings, pillow covers and cushions, book covers, table covers and carpets. It is from this period and its development to the present day that twentieth century work has evolved. Some wonderful stitches developed in the eighteenth century, as shown in the Hatton Garden hangings at the Victoria and Albert Museum. The nineteenth century saw a flood of Berlin wool work designs and aniline-dyed wool for working them, including footstools, prie-dieus and gentlemen's slippers.

From the 1960s to the present day many hundreds of stitches have been developed, named and renamed, whilst petit point and gros point (pronounced in the French way) have been quite overwhelmed by Florentine patterns, now renamed Bargello. This is one of the easiest types of work for the less experienced worker. It involves quite a lot of 'needle pushing' once a decision has been made on colours and the pattern to follow. There have also been a number of cushion and other kits designed and sold through newspapers and magazines.

Background material and yarns are reasonably easy to obtain. Most towns now have at least one craft shop selling evenweave material or canvas suitable for the work. Quality of canvas varies and it is best judged by holding to the light to see how much dressing it contains. If the worker has reasonably cool hands, does not pull the canvas out of shape too easily and uses suitable thickness of yarn, a cheap canvas, although usually containing more dressing, will suffice. However, articles that need good wearing properties must be of the best quality the user can afford. A white canvas, because of bleaching, is considered weaker than a natural one.

Kneelers and cushions should have careful consideration as far as materials are concerned, as church furnishings, particularly, are expected to last an extremely long time and they can get a lot of hard wear.

The choice of size of canvas depends on the purpose for which the article is to be worked and on the eyesight and ability of the worker. Canvas can be as fine as 22 holes to $2\frac{1}{2}$cm (1in) through to rug canvas, which is also quite suitable for stitching; but 16s or 14s are a reasonable starting point for the beginner.

Assuming the worker has size 16s canvas for experimental purposes, Appleton's crewel wool will give a large range of colour, and three strands in the needle adequately fills the canvas when using many stitches. On becoming more proficient there are many other yarns the worker can try. Knitting wool can be somewhat restricting in colour, tends to be rather soft and could be expensive. Embroidery cottons, silks and other yarns can create lovely effects; trials will soon confirm the suitability of the choice. Interesting additions to the work could be leather, beads, sequins or gold thread work, bearing in mind that beads would be uncomfortable on a kneeler!

Tapestry needles are the correct ones to use. These have a large eye and a blunt point. The size of needle depends on the canvas. A rule of thumb is that if the canvas just holds a needle and the yarn fits easily through the eye, the needle is the correct size. With very large mesh canvas there may be difficulties in obtaining a needle, but knitting needle packs sometimes have a suitable one. It is advisable to thread the needle with short lengths of yarn, otherwise it can be worn thin by the canvas, resulting in an uneven appearance.

There are many books published showing numerous stitches of various textures and shapes, but basically the art of canvas work is to cover a grid system. There are three ways of doing this: horizontally, vertically and diagonally; and when a horizontal stitch is laid over a vertical, or diagonals over each other, the result is a cross. From then on, inventiveness can take over.

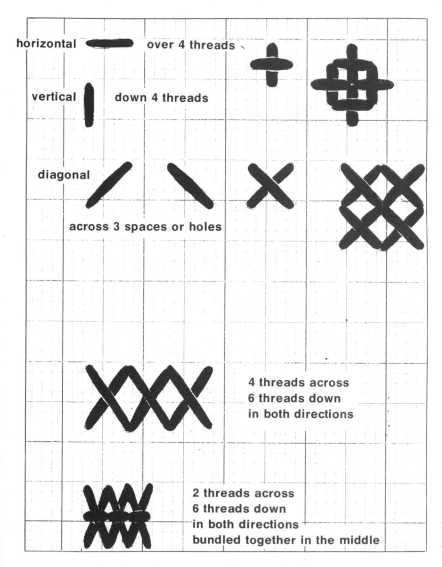

horizontal ▬ over 4 threads

vertical ▌ down 4 threads

diagonal

across 3 spaces or holes

4 threads across
6 threads down
in both directions

2 threads across
6 threads down
in both directions
bundled together in the middle

A diagram of canvas work grid system. It is difficult to decide whether to count threads or holes of the canvas. Hundreds of stitches can be created by understanding these few diagrams

6 threads down

**1 across
6 threads down**

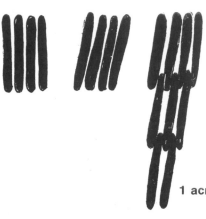

**1 across 6 threads down
encroaching**

**2 across
6 down**

**3 across
6 down**

Further developments to the grid
system

Further developments showing
Bargello or Florentine style

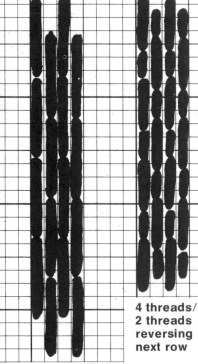

**each stitch
over 6 threads
second row begins
3 threads down**

**4 threads/
2 threads
reversing
next row**

**3 threads
dropping one
thread at
beginning of
each row**

**3 threads
each row
dropping one
thread for row
two and up
again for row
three**

**4 threads each
row, dropping
two each row
for the first stitch**

**4 threads each
stitch. Second
row starts at
dropping one.
Same third row
but reversing for
and five which
makes it level w
first row. Repea**

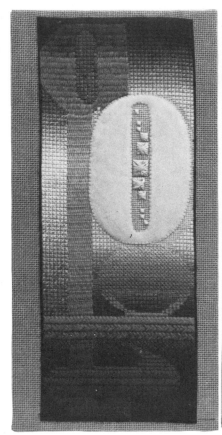

Canvas panels showing shading and
applied leather 'Name, address
panels designed for the sides of a
tote bag'. Left, 90 BHL; right, MCSh

There are two major considerations in canvas work. One is texture, the other
shading; and for something very alive and busy these can be combined. It is
also a very suitable medium in which to work letters, being particularly suited
to straight letters and creating an interesting shape, because of the diagonals,
in curved ones. Letters can also be applied, in leather or material, straight onto
the canvas and stitches worked up to the edge of the applied material.
Freehand stitches, such as straight stitch or chain stitch, can be added over the
top of canvas stitches for an enhanced effect.

When designing for canvas work its angularity must be respected and
accepted, but not pandered to. There are several well tried methods of
designing, such as carefully drawing and marking out on graph paper, then
counting squares from the graph onto the canvas while working. This method
can hinder creativity and become rather boring in execution. So normal
methods of designing, using cut paper, pens, pencils and paints on paper,
should be carried out. The design is quite simply traced onto the canvas with a
fibre-tip pen which is manufactured for this purpose. Ordinary water-ink fibre
tips could run when the work is stretched, and waterproof ones could rot the
canvas, whilst pencil is inclined to rub off and soil the yarns. Some canvas is
difficult to see through and therefore the main outline of the design should be a
heavy black line.

Care must be taken that straight lines of the lettering coincide exactly with
the threads of the canvas. Thick uprights can be embellished with more than
one stitch or the whole letter can be worked in a simple tent or cross stitch with
the background enriched with shading and different stitches, thereby emphasising the letter.

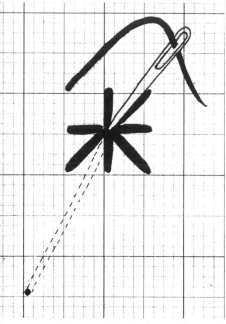

as far as possible bring the needle up in the background and take it down against the previous work

when beginning and ending off threads make a knot in the yarn; take the needle through from the right side a short distance away from the work so that as it lies on the wrong side it will be stitched over. The thread should be brought to the right side and stitched over when it has completed its job

Diagram of beginning, ending and working methods of canvas work

stretching canvas work.

1. Place to tack at each end of one edge, checking that the edge measures the same distance from the edge of the board
2. Put tacks in side one, then side two, then side three
3. Pull firmly to get the fourth edge in position

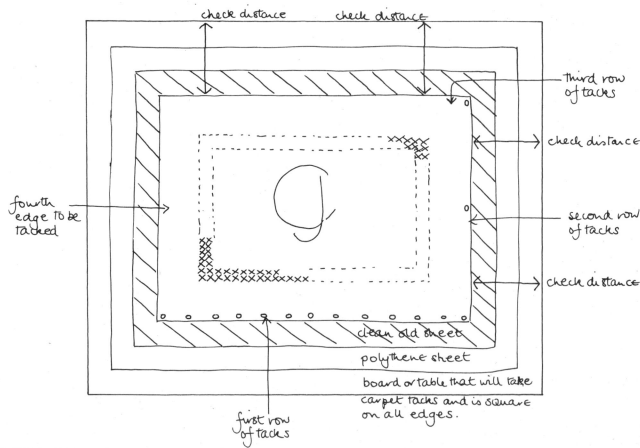

A slate frame is not essential for canvas work. With large pieces of work it is easier to roll the embroidery from one side of the frame to the other on completion, but it is difficult to see the work as a whole and the frame is more awkward to carry around. It really is a question of preference.

Whenever possible, when working stitches, the needle should be brought up into the canvas and taken back into the previous work. This creates a pitted

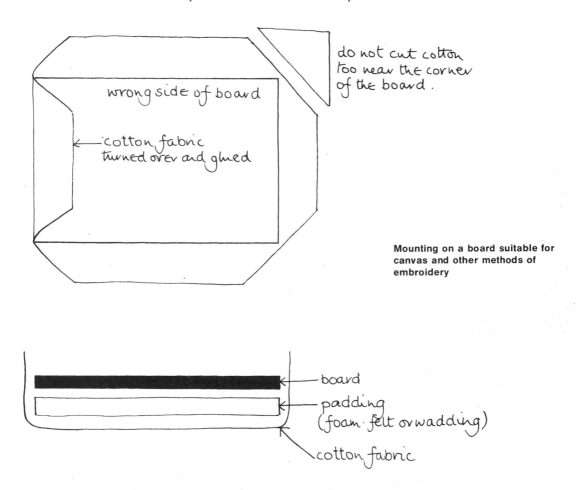

do not cut cotton too near the corner of the board.

wrong side of board

cotton fabric turned over and glued

Mounting on a board suitable for canvas and other methods of embroidery

board

padding (foam · felt or wadding)

cotton fabric

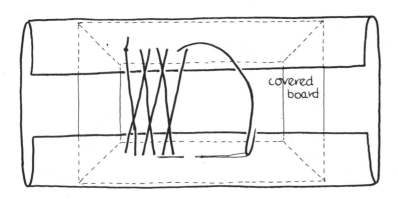

covered board

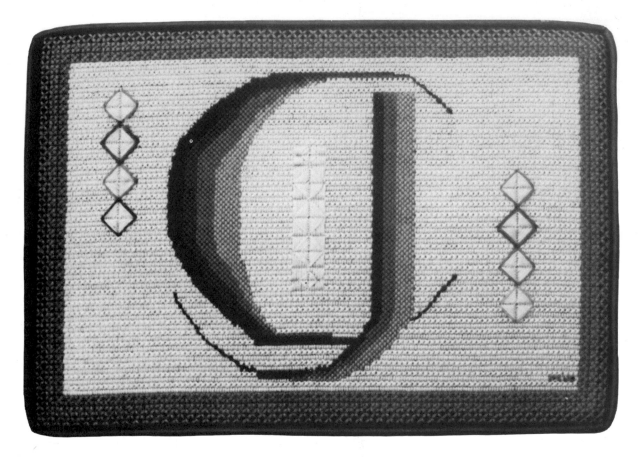

One of a pair of wedding kneelers featuring the initials of the bride and groom

look, adding to the textural qualities, whereas bringing yarn through the canvas beside previous stitches tends to bring up fluff, thereby obscuring the hole.

When the work is complete it is sensible to do two rows of cross stitch around the edge so that sewing up or mounting stitches can grip to this, otherwise the canvas may just unravel. The edges can also become unravelled if held in the hand while working, but this can be prevented by using masking tape, by oversewing all round or using some other temporary protection.

If the work contains no materials that run or would be affected by water it should, on completion, be stretched, using a wet method (see diagram). If, however, it incorporates gold thread or leather, which should under no circumstances be dampened, it is best to pin out and leave it for several days without damping.

For making up, if it is to be a picture for a wall, it should be treated as other pictures, stretched onto a board with lacing and then either framed or mounted onto a fabric covered second board. But canvas work is very suitable for many articles such as jewellery boxes, pincushions, spectacle cases, day and evening bags, purses, collars, belts, necklaces, book-binding, door plates, cushions, chairseats, waistcoats, mirror and picture frames, children's toy boxes, and many more. A very versatile technique!

Canvas work, Jennifer Gray, Batsford, 1974
Needlepoint, Mary Rhodes, Octopus Books, 1974
Filling Stitches, Edith John, Batsford, 1967

5 Blackwork

There are many explanations as to where blackwork came from and why it was so called. Various examples still survive. There are Elizabethan caps, jackets and shirts decorated in monochrome seeding patterns, and embroidered shapes outlined with additional metal thread decoration, and they resemble the twentieth century effect in spite of their different method of working!

Twentieth century blackwork consists of simple or intricate patterns worked on evenweave fabric in black or in colour. The edges of the design can be, but are not necessarily, embroidered in a smooth stitch such as whipped chain or stem stitch. The work has been used for panels and pictures, box covers, needlebooks and book covers, as well as table linen.

There are various grades of evenweave linen, coarse and fine, and yarns of all sorts from fine man-made sewing thread to stranded silk or cotton, various linen threads and smooth weaving yarns.

The greatest tonal contrast is black on white, which is rather stark, so, if using the work in the twentieth century tradition, a natural linen fabric is

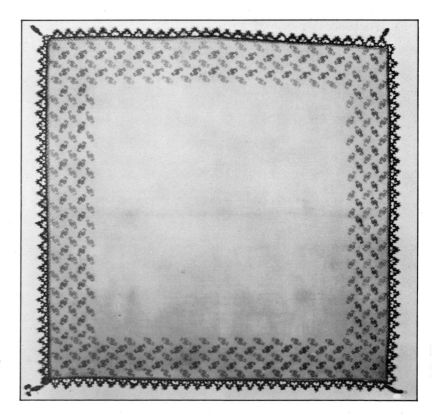

An embroidered handkerchief, worked in Holbein stitch in the late sixteenth and early seventeenth century. The small S-shaped motifs are worked in pale green and yellow silk; but this is an example of the effect created by some method of small straight stitches

Blackwork patterns worked out on
squared paper

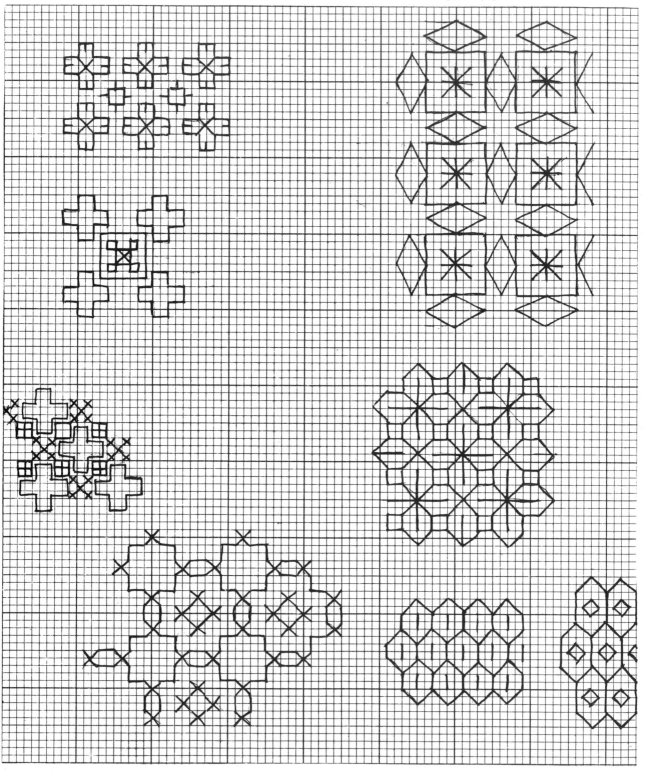

better. As soon as colour is introduced the tonal contrast is lessened. Yarns can be of various thicknesses in one piece of work; the thicker the yarn the darker the tone, because of denser patterning. If stranded yarn is used there need be no greater variation than increasing or decreasing the strands; or the same thickness of yarn can be used throughout.

When employing this work for lettering it can be used in two major ways. One is by working the background and letters in different patterns; the other is by only working the background or only working the letters.

The design should be placed on the material by tracing onto tissue paper, placing the paper in position, tacking essential lines and then tearing away the paper.

Blackwork is suitable for such articles as table linen, bed linen, patterns of letters on children's clothing, curtain hems and commemorative work.

It must be remembered that, for table linen or work that could be washed frequently, the back should be extremely neat, otherwise the iron will get caught in the threads and therefore ruin the work. Some man-made yarns need to be ironed at a cool temperature and this should be considered when working on linen which requires laundering, and a hot iron.

There is an upsurge of interest in needlepoint lace. This lace makes interesting edges to articles or garments decorated in blackwork patterns. Traditionally, it was worked in metal thread around the hem of articles such as handkerchiefs and coifs and is complementary to this delicate type of work.

Blackwork Embroidery, Geddes/McNeill, Dover Publications, 1976

6 Cross stitch and double running

A type of cross stitch called Assissi work has the background covered with crosses leaving the subject void. This method of voiding is very suitable for lettering, particularly for working alphabets for children, as the background fabric can have lots of colour applied. The letters can be very clearly defined.

The background material for cross stitch should be an evenweave fabric of a kind with the same number of threads to the centimetre both warp and weft ways. There are several specialist materials available in embroidery supply shops. Careful hunting may reveal suitable materials in either dress or furnishing fabric departments. Should some fabric be chosen which is of a very smooth quality, offering itself as highly suitable for the purpose but not very satisfactory for cross stitch, it is possible to tack canvas of appropriate size

An example of voiding, in this case using cross stitch

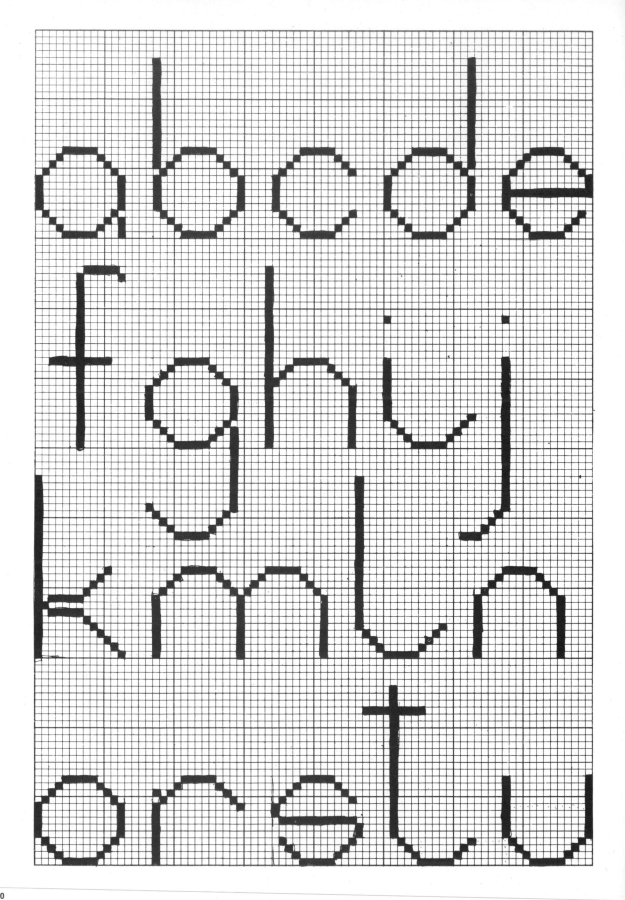

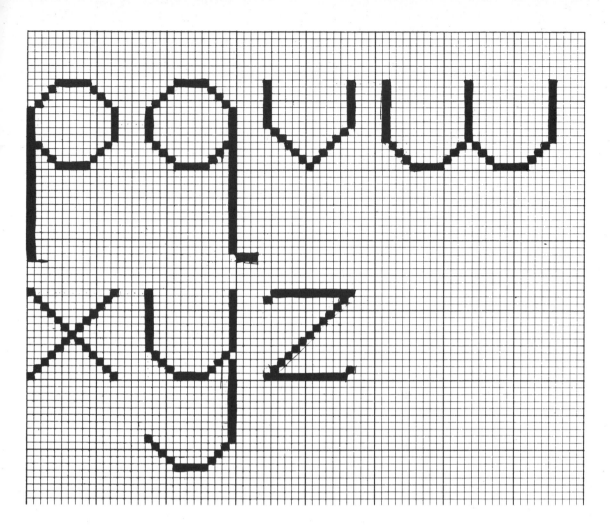

An alphabet designed using a square of thirteen spaces

onto the material and work over the canvas as a guide line. The canvas is then pulled out on completion of the work.

Stitching yarns can be any yarn that is suitable for the fabric and the size of stitch. The thread should go through the material with reasonable ease and the finished stitch should look full, not mean, unless a very spidery effect is required, when it should be really thin to be as effective as possible.

Cross stitch alphabets are very fascinating to design. This is easiest using squared paper. It is probably the easiest form of lettering for the embroiderer to design (see the alphabet illustrated). The design is not transferred onto the material. The position can be marked with tacking and you may need to work the design from the centre outwards rather than spend a long time counting out threads. If the work is started from a side margin then obviously this is where to begin. A calculation needs to be made so that the final line does not come too low on the fabric.

Cross stitch can be worked easily in the hand, although a frame is not unsuitable.

Double running can be used for lettering but its more important role is one of supporting the design of the cross stitch. Many fascinating patterns can be devised using this stitch, which is attractive on both sides of the fabric. It also is designed on squared paper.

Articles like curtains decorated in cross stitch look additionally attractive with tassels and fringes. The peasant-type work lends itself to decorative edges, using the background fabric.

Anchor Manual of Needlework, Batsford, 1958

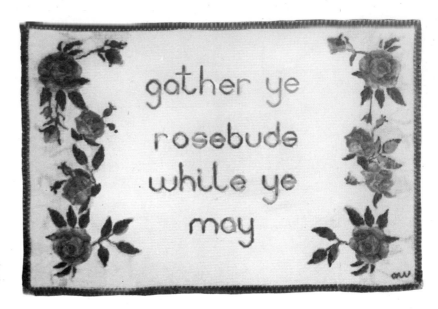

Picture using the alphabet designed on squared paper from the previous illustration

Positioning of letters for a poem, sentence or phrase

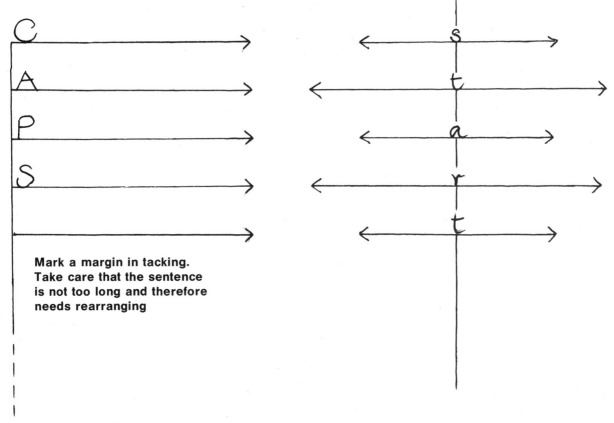

Mark a margin in tacking. Take care that the sentence is not too long and therefore needs rearranging

Consider this way

find the centre of sentence counting the space between words as one letter

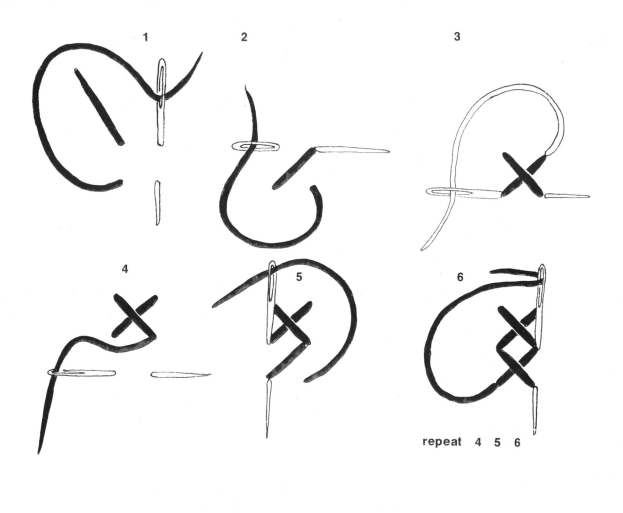

1 2 3

4 5 6

repeat 4 5 6

Backview

Marking cross stitch

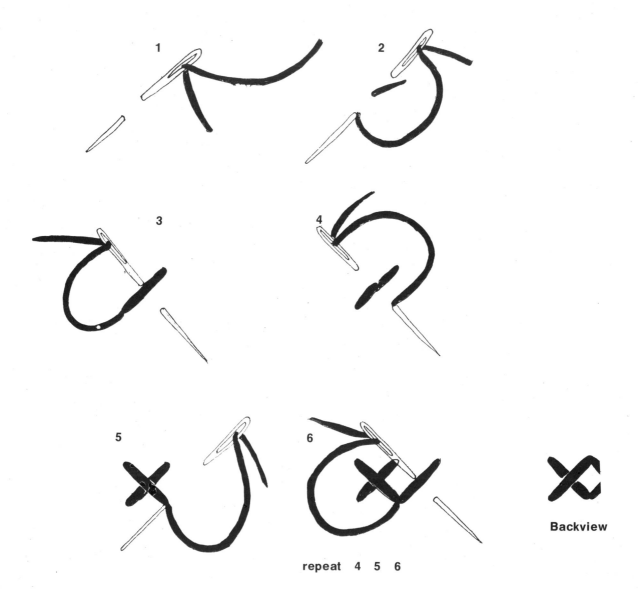

repeat 4 5 6

Backview

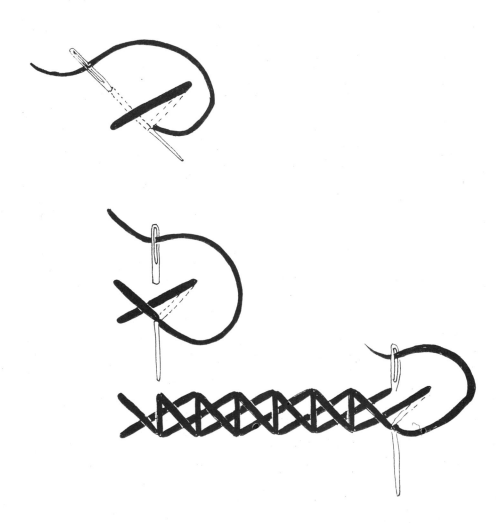

Algerian eye

Cross stitch and double running

Double running stitch

Nineteenth century sampler showing use of Algerian eye and cross stitch

7 Freehand stitches

There is difficulty in knowing where to begin and where to end on the subject of freehand stitches. So many types of work are freehand stitches which then become part of that technique.

A vast knowledge of many different stitches cannot be considered an advantage if the embroiderer is incapable of applying them satisfactorily to suit a particular requirement. The classic books on stitches group them into families in different ways. Mrs Archibald Christie refers to 'flat, looped, chained and knotted stitches and composite stitches which combine more than one', whilst Constance Howard describes stitches as being 'flat, raised, looped or knotted. Two or even three may be combined to make a new one.' These two books were published sixty years apart; both have similar aims but different presentation.

It is useful to know a small vocabulary of stitches. These can be used in various weight yarns, in different sizes. Spacing and combining of rows of

Section from a bedspread. A red and white patchwork bedspread, dated 1913. Worked by customers for the proprietor of the King's Head, Norton, Gloucestershire

stitches are interesting exercises in basic design and these can easily be turned into letters.

Different stitches present different effects, viz:

Wide solid – plaited braid stitch; Romanian stitch.
Wide spiky – thorn stitch; Cretan stitch.
Smooth solid – rope stitch.
Knotted solid – knotted chain.
Fine line – split stitch; stem stitch.

Most fabrics are suitable and also most yarns. The field is very wide and the use very varied. When lettering is to be applied to a garment – for example, a teenager's name to her blouse – considerations should be whether the yarn is too thick or too thin for the weight of the fabric and whether both have the same washing properties. For example, don't use a thick wool yarn on a thin silk shirt. The needle needed for the wool would distort and damage the silk and the wool would tend to gather up on being washed on a light fabric.

Similarly, size of stitch should be considered and a smooth stitch chosen for a joined-up name; whipped chain stitch, perhaps, using two lines for the capitals, would be very suitable.

A stitch which works very successfully in capital letters for something such

A roll embroidered with signatures presented to Edith John on her retirement. There are a number of line stitches suitable for embroidered names, such as chain, whipped chain, stem, split, back stitch, whipped back stitch

as a church banner, a children's panel or a tablecloth is raised chain band. If a suitable yarn is chosen this can work particularly well, even for the inexperienced embroiderer. It is also quick to do compared with some methods.

When writing about lettering it is difficult to make suggestions as to where to use it, as the situation is usually created and the freehand stitches chosen specifically for a particular job.

Embroidery, Nora Jones, Macdonald Guidelines
Creative Stitchery, Dona Z Meilach/Lee Erlin Snow, Pitman, 1967
The Constance Howard Book of Stitches, Batsford, 1979

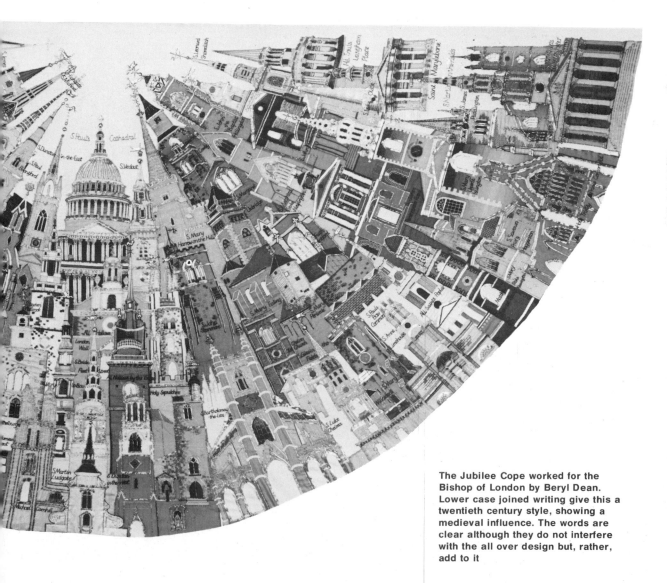

The Jubilee Cope worked for the Bishop of London by Beryl Dean. Lower case joined writing give this a twentieth century style, showing a medieval influence. The words are clear although they do not interfere with the all over design but, rather, add to it

There is an interesting use of texture on this W. Stitches include cretan, french knots, beads and sequins and rosette chain edging

Freehand stitches and applique combined to create this delightful panel for a chapel in Salisbury Cathedral

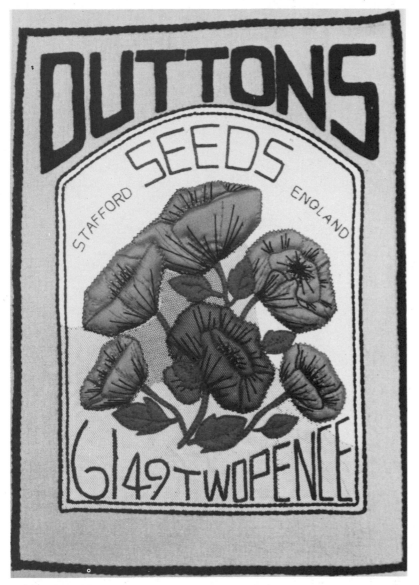

A design for a panel, the lettering playing a vital role in the overall finished effect

A box, twice the width of a penny, embroidered 'M' with bullion stitch roses. A delightful box in which to keep a special ring or ear rings

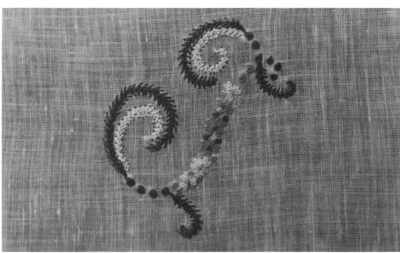

A handkerchief purchased from a shop, showing hand embroidery worked commercially but interestingly created. It is interesting to speculate how long one of these takes to work and how much the embroiderer is paid

Freehand stitches

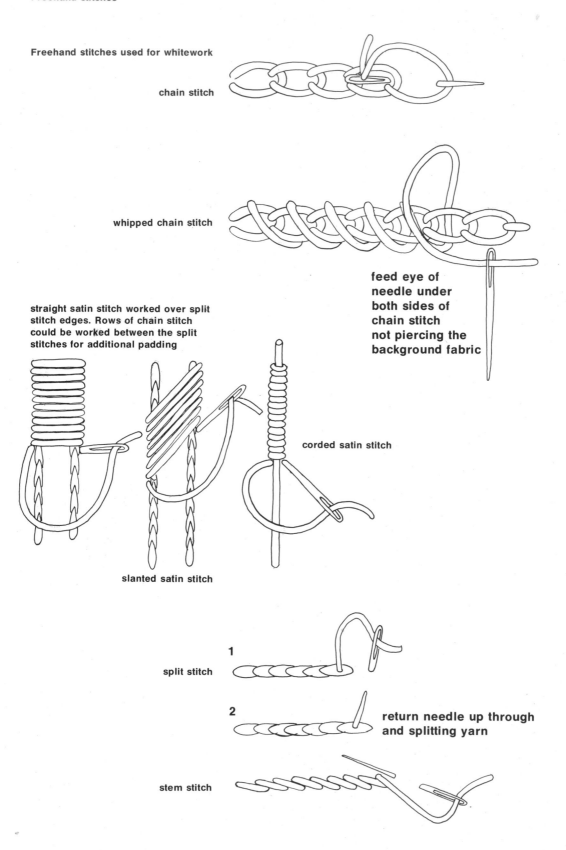

Freehand stitches used for whitework

chain stitch

whipped chain stitch

**feed eye of
needle under
both sides of
chain stitch
not piercing the
background fabric**

straight satin stitch worked over split
stitch edges. Rows of chain stitch
could be worked between the split
stitches for additional padding

corded satin stitch

slanted satin stitch

split stitch

1

2

**return needle up through
and splitting yarn**

stem stitch

8 Whitework

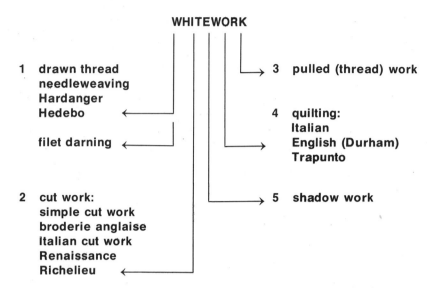

WHITEWORK

1   **drawn thread
needleweaving
Hardanger
Hedebo**

     filet darning

2   **cut work:
simple cut work
broderie anglaise
Italian cut work
Renaissance
Richelieu**

3   **pulled (thread) work**

4   **quilting:
Italian
English (Durham)
Trapunto**

5   **shadow work**

The question of the use of whitework lettering should be considered before embarking on pieces of work. Alphabets were frequently featured in women's magazines of the nineteenth century and many family book shelves in a home where there has been a long and lively interest in embroidery contain a copy of Dillmont. Who better to teach the Victorian way of monogramming handkerchiefs, nightwear, underwear, table linen and bed linen? Even a royal crown is included in the instructions – would this symbol be in common use? So, these are places where whitework embroidery has been used. But what is whitework embroidery and where can it be used today?

There are numerous forms of whitework (as shown by the 'family tree' diagram) originating in many different countries of the world. Sometimes a form of whitework has come to be more closely associated with the country into which it has been imported, perhaps by a missionary, than with its country of origin. Ayrshire work was developed by Mrs Jamieson of Ayr who was lent a French christening robe, inset with lace stitches, in 1814. According to Margaret Swain (author of *The Flowerers*), Mrs Jamieson copied the fillings and also taught them. She was already an agent for embroidery. It gradually evolved its own style and in its way became more delicate than the original. Part of its evolution is due to the use to which it was put.

The five main groups of work consist of:

1   Threads withdrawn in lines warp way and weft way or both, with the remaining threads then grouped together and darning patterns worked over them.

2   Cut work, when a shape unrelated to the threads of the material is stitched round to prevent fraying and then parts of the background cut away.

3   Background linen fabric is stitched with a matching thread in a pattern and the threads are pulled tightly, giving the background fabric a characteristic patterned look.

Letters from a magazine of 1860.
Were the hatching marks an
indication of the direction of the top
row of satin stitch?

4   Background fabric is stitched with a matching thread in a design and the fabric is padded in some way to create shadows on the surface, therefore enhancing the pattern.

5   The design is stitched on transparent fabric on the wrong side, creating shadows on the right side.

The characteristic of whitework is its atonal quality. It depends on the fall of light for interest, giving very white, grey and dark grey areas. Satin stitch is very light, patterns grey and cut or drawn areas dark grey.

Other methods exploiting this atonal quality include quilting, net and filet darning, shadow work and soutache braid. The differences between whitework and lace worked with a needle are often very slight, particularly when referring to insertion stitches.

Linen is the principal background material for whitework, linen thread the major yarn. By its very nature and colour and uses to which it is put, it is a work that requires frequent washing. Linen, stronger when wet, is very suitable for the work; it keeps its colour, can be boiled and if the work is in very fine yarns these are more likely to stand up to laundry strains. Whitework was used in the past to decorate household linen, tablecloths, pillowcases, handkerchiefs, collars and cuffs and other articles and garments very vulnerable to dirt.

To suggest a supplier or a particular type of linen background depends a great deal on fashion of the moment, success of the flax crop and popularity of the subject. Use of whatever is available will help the needlewoman to discriminate between the worthwhile and the material that is a timewaster. Exclusive shops, or market stalls, often produce a surprising fabric. The revival of bobbin lace making has made white linen yarn much more readily available. The late 1970s/early 1980s revival of silk blouses could progress to linen ones and then every fabric store would stock this material. Such methods as hardanger require specialist fabric as the material used is a hopsack weave. It also requires only two weights of yarn for stitching and generally cotton perle is used – a smooth shining yarn, heavy for the kloster blocks and fine for the weaving in the withdrawn areas. This work can also be done in colour, as can several whitework methods, the worker deciding which is preferred. Pulled stitches require an open weave which is even, fairly close weave for drawn work and close for cut work.

Bearing in mind that, with continuous use, cotton can lose its whiteness it can, nevertheless, be used on the whitework and should not be excluded.

It is not proposed, here, to show all types of whitework as lettering is the interest. One of the types of whitework which could include lettering design is drawn work, which often features areas of patterning within the withdrawn areas. Drawn work, basically, is a very elaborate hem.

Renaissance, Richelieu, broderie anglaise, are but a few of the many styles of cut work. Often the difference between one and another is very slight and should not be the concern of the worker trying out experiments. The main differences are the treatment of the cut edge, either buttonhole or oversewing, and the use of brides, which are the worked bars joining the remaining fabric pieces.

Make a careful study of the traditional form of the techniques and the way that the type of embroidery can be fitted to letter forms. By the very nature of withdrawing threads, drawn work is angular, the lines following the warp and weft of the material. Satin stitch is worked with drawn work and this stitch can help out when curved areas are required. Slanted satin stitch curves better than straight satin stitch.

Cut work is a curvaceous style of work, so an appropriate alphabet should be

Monograms from mid-nineteenth century magazines

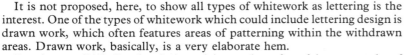

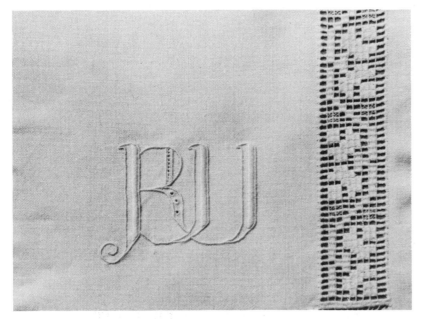

Monogram worked in 1959 as part of the training of the Royal School of Needlework. The uprights of the letters have been split so that the satin stitch is not too wide and the letter becomes more interesting

A recently purchased handkerchief, probably Italian. It seems a pity that these delightful pieces of work have the design marked out so densely

chosen, such as lettering based on Celtic words. Do not forget to have enough background material to support the shape – and the space between!

Pulled thread work needs chunky areas to show to advantage the interesting pulled fabric and the complementary surface stitched patterns.

Anchor Manual of Needlework, Batsford, 1958

9 Needlepoint lace

There are two main forms of lace making. One is made by a type of plaiting using bobbins to hold the thread taut and the other is a satellite form of embroidery using a needle creating small buttonhole type stitches.

Needlemade lace originated in Italy during the sixteenth century. The earliest work was the Reticella lace, openwork linen thread patterns of a geometric nature. It has a complex history and development, becoming a freer form of work based on floral form called Venetian point. It is exquisite work using very fine thread producing beautiful textures.

There have been revivals of the work over the centuries, particularly in the last century in Italy and in the mid-twentieth century. A revival of lace in general may well lead once more to interesting and lovely work, gathering together the best and most satisfying stitches and creating new styles of design.

There is no background fabric to the lace as the stitching creates the fabric. The motif can be inserted into or surrounded by fabric, the type of material depending on the purpose for which it is required. The yarn should be as fine as the worker can cope with, if this is to be worked to create something very delicate. It is interesting to use it on a different scale, in which case the yarn should be firm and hold its shape. The design is traced onto firm paper or thin card and then tacked. A raised and thickened edge is worked over the tacking

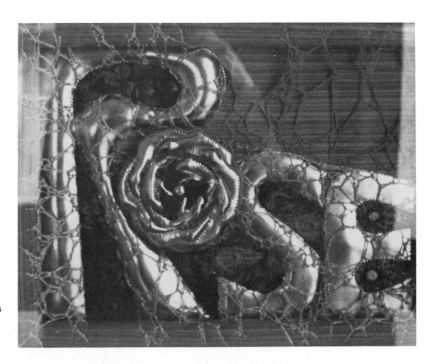

'ROSE' worked in kid and thin fabrics supported by needlepoint or buttonhole stitch fillings. It was then mounted and framed

by buttonholing over a third cord. This gives the foundation onto which the filling stitches are attached.

There are so many different filling stitches that it is very difficult to do justice to needlepoint lace briefly. Should the method of work appeal to the reader, there are one or two new books already on the market. The interesting needlepoint patterns make very fascinating fillings for capital letters when the shape of the letter is broken up.

Needlelace and Needleweaving, Jill Nordfors, Van Nostrand Reinhold, 1974

The Technique of Needlepoint Lace, Nenia Lovesey, Batsford, 1980

Needleweaving, Edith John, Batsford, 1970

10 Shadow work

Shadow work is a very delicate method of creating a design on transparent or opaque fabric. It can be worked in monochrome or in colour or perhaps gently contrasting shades such as pale blue on white.

There are a number of suitable fabrics, both man-made and natural, which include cotton lawn, polycotton and nylon organza. The laundering requirements are one of the main considerations when choosing materials; the stitching yarn should be similar to the background fabric in type, otherwise there can be problems with quick as opposed to slow drying properties.

There are two main stitches: one is double back stitch, the other herringbone. These stitches are worked on the wrong side, which increases the colour on the right side. Fabric can be applied and used in conjunction with the stitching, as well as punch stitch, eyelets, stem stitch and satin stitch.

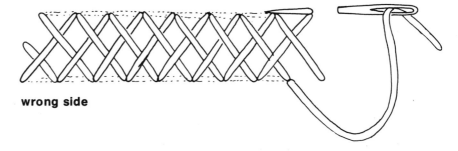

wrong side

right side

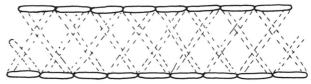

Shadow work diagram of double back stitch

Shadow work is very suitable for those articles that require pale, diaphanous material, particularly for ceremonial occasions. It lends itself well to letter shapes. It could be used to decorate the scarf around a hat at the races, or a wedding; or perhaps for a stole, as both sides are very neat.

The design can, in most cases, be traced onto the material with a very hard pencil. If this is not possible, paper with the design on it can be tacked to the right side of the material and the herringbone stitch worked from the wrong side following the design on the paper.

A rolled hem, punch stitch or pin stitch is suitable for the edge and fits in with the style of work.

Anchor Manual of Needlework, Batsford, 1958

II Soutache

A form of needlework that has long since departed from the fashion scene is soutache embroidery. There is a very fine example of an alphabet which is suitable for soutache in Dillmont's *Encyclopaedia of Needlework* which was designed by Giovan' Antonio Tagliente and published in Venice in 1562.

Soutache embroidery consists of using a braid which is twined and threaded through itself and held down with small stitches. The braid is of plaited construction which enables it to curve easily. The alphabet and the braid are only a starting point for experimentation as it appears to be a quick decorative method of surface work which would lend itself to lots of further ornamentation; it could be worked very small, from 2.5cm (1in), right up to 18 or 20cm (7 or 8in). The width of the braid should be in proportion to the size of the letter. A braid could be made either by plaiting or finger weaving, this being preferable to a purchased braid as it could be made in the texture and colour suitable for the work, or to the worker's choice. A soft cotton yarn or fine wool are good starting threads for making the braid. The background fabric would be suited to its purpose and the lettering and fabric should then work well together.

Small running stitches would hold the braid in place. Additional embroidery would depend on the purpose of the lettering. Large wall coverings could be made in thick woollen fabric and the braid made from carpet thrums, and further decoration with applied shapes, perhaps in relief, made of felt or other fabrics stitched round with machine satin stitch to prevent fraying.

This lettering would be very suitable for children's alphabet books, with soutache-style capitals and a chain, whipped chain or other freehand stitch with a plait-like quality used for lower case letters.

Encyclopedia of Needlework, Th. de Dillmont, DMC, Mulhouse, France, 1897

A soutache letter after Dillmont. A surface decoration. The braid for the letter is secured temporarily and the Arabic pattern interwoven in a thinner braid, cord or plait. The braid of the 'A' shape is then filled with a needlepoint lace filling after the braid has been firmly stitched down

Monogram JPW influenced by Guilloche stitch, soutache braid and computer lettering

a.

1 2 3 4

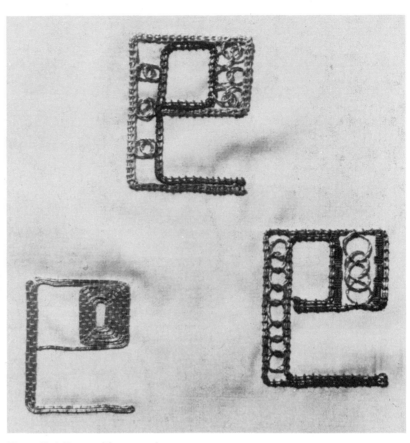

Three Es influenced by computer lettering

1
2 3
4

Diagrams to show plaiting and finger weaving. (a) One over two, three over four. Renumber one, two, three, four. Two over three. Repeat

8 7 6 5 4 3 2 1

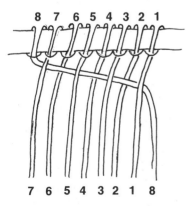

7 6 5 4 3 2 1 8

8 7 6 5 4 3 2 1

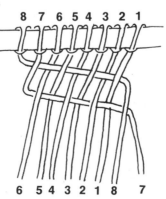

6 5 4 3 2 1 8 7

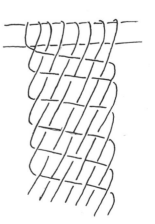

12 Quilting

Quilting is the decorative way of stitching together two or more layers of fabric. The purpose of the finished work is usually one of protection, perhaps against cold; in earlier centuries it was also worn as padding underneath armour. Quilted jackets are in great demand today and are made commercially in large quantities. It makes a bed cover, household article or garment very individual if it includes a monogram or even the whole name of the user.

There are several kinds of quilting, the three main kinds being English, Italian and Trapunto. There is another work known as shadow quilting but this is really a form of shadow work using fabric to create the shadowed colour changes instead of stitches.

English (Durham) quilting consists of a three layer sandwich. A pattern is created on the top surface by stitching through the middle padding layer and the lining, making decorative lines with running stitches.

Italian quilting is a corded decoration where two layers are stitched with a double row of running stitches, thus creating a channel which is threaded from the wrong side with wool and therefore stands out.

Trapunto quilting consists of two layers stitched together with back stitch. The shapes are complete and are then padded from behind by cutting a hole in the back material, pushing in the padding and stitching together again.

All three methods and shadow quilting are suitable for lettering.

Materials for quilting should be of a firm nature and one that creates shadows, as this is where the beauty of the work lies. A luxurious quality of work is obtained by using silk, particularly natural-coloured; for example, shantung, crêpe de Chine, or some weight of silk between these two. Wool/cotton mixtures such as Viyella work very well, but the choice of material depends mainly on its final use. Cotton lawn or polycotton are suitable for the article requiring frequent washing, while poplin is preferable where a larger area is being covered with quilting as this is a firmer fabric.

The padding can be teased fleece, or even an old blanket. Synthetic wadding is more suitable with man-made materials, resulting in an easily-washed article.

Stitching yarns need to be firm and not too fine or they will pinch the fabric, rather than holding it firmly and letting it swell around, thus creating the soft, undulating mounds which characterize this beautiful work.

The running stitches for the English and Italian quilting should be very even. The article could be completely reversible and therefore the length of both the stitch and the gap in between should be equal on both sides.

Bed quilts traditionally were made on frames and were worked by gathering several stitches onto the needle before pulling the yarn through; this was obviously a great skill.

Trapunto quilting is back-stitched around the edge of the design. The padding is inserted from behind through a cut hole which is repaired with herring bone stitch. The back stitch does not have to cope with great thicknesses of padding.

When designing for English quilting it must be remembered that the purpose of the stitches is primarily to hold three layers together; therefore the

A quilted book cover made in suede with little secret gardens embroidered in the spaces between the letters

stitching should leave fairly equal areas in between. If large areas are left with no stitching the filling could, if it were something like fleece, start shifting around and could become lumpy.

There are so many ways that lettering could be used in English quilting. The letters could be worked in rows, going around a square, back to front – the possibilities are endless. Both capitals and lower case letters would be suitable; depending on the article, a name could be worked, a motto, an address or a greeting.

Italian quilting lends itself admirably to lower case joined writing. Perhaps a cushion with a message across it, with a more traditional border; or a teenager's housecoat or bedroom cushions decorated with her own or her favourite pop-star's name or initials.

Trapunto capital letters could be used to advantage rather after the style of the Victorian monogram. The additional lines would be in backstitch, that is where the fabric is not double.

A quilting frame is essential for working as the needle needs to go down through and back up through the work in one movement. Quilting is not framed taut as is most other work. Because of the size of some articles, rollers form the sides of the frame, allowing the work to be easily moved across as it progresses. Some of these frames have to be large enough to accommodate a bedspread; fortunately, quilting frames have a ratchet system for moving the rollers, in place of the more usual pegs and side-slats of smaller frames.

A short needle (a between needle) is preferred by some workers, the size depending on the yarn and the fabric used.

Traditionally the design was transferred onto the material by means of drawing with the eye of the needle around a template. There is now available a pen that marks fabric with a substance which disappears on contact with water. For the most delicate fabrics, which presumably will be for small articles, the design should be transferred onto tracing paper with a waterproof pen and then the design tacked into position and the quilting worked through all layers.

A very satisfactory finish to a quilted edge is binding; this is both neat and in keeping with the type of work.

Articles that can be made include a cosmetic bag, a child's garment, perhaps quilted around the hem, a pram or cot quilt, a bed cover or cushions.

Quilting, Ed. Kit Pyman, Search Press, 1978

Quilting, Eirian Short, Batsford, 1981

13 Machine embroidery

The principles of the sewing machine were invented during the eighteenth century but the machine was not put into production until well into the nineteenth century.

Barthelemy Thimonnier, a Frenchman, set up a factory to make machines in 1845, but it is not known whether he actually produced and sold any. However, by the mid-1850s other manufacturers succeeded, and sewing machines were being sold in many parts of the world. An adapted industrial sewing machine has been used for embroidery for much longer than the domestic type, although edging or top-stitching has been practised as long as machines have been used for sewing seams.

The raised textures that a domestic sewing machine can produce, and the aids to applique, have been generally accepted since their development in the 1950s, being part of the revival of embroidery of the post-war scene. There have been makes of machine produced with built-in patterns. The use of the machine for applique work is dealt with in Chapter 14.

With the foot in position, machine lines creating lettering can be used on most fabrics and also on leather; similarly, for quilting, using two or more layers of fabric. The machine will take a thick and thin yarn, the thick being placed in the bobbin. Yarns too thick for the bobbin can be applied with a zigzag or straight stitch and some machines have a foot modified for this purpose.

Linear stitches can be created freehand with the foot taken off and the teeth or feed dog covered or dropped. The lines are then worked on material which is mounted in a shallow round frame. The needle is in a fixed position and is treated as though it were the pencil inscribing on the moving fabric.

Using the same method, a sewing machine which is adapted to zigzagging can create a different kind of lettering. The stitch width dial can be adjusted to produce several widths; the widest, when applied to lettering, giving a larger scale and consequently being more suitable for upper case lettering. Marion Richardson's round hand style of writing (as taught to school children) or, indeed, any round form of joined-up lettering works well, particularly when enhanced by figure-of-eight-style decoration; also, other simple designs, such as writing patterns taught to young children. Italic-style writing, however, creates difficulties. The zigzag capitals form good monograms, making full use of diagonals creating thick and thin lines. There are a number of texture patterns that can be worked by the machine, and these can be used to infill letter shapes. The built-in machine patterns can be used either to infill or create letters.

Background fabrics for freehand machine embroidery need to be of a medium or light weight and they need to be strong. Cotton lawn or poplin, thin wool/cotton mixtures (Viyella) or polycotton are suitable for beginners. Of course, these are not the only fabrics that can be used but skill should be practised on these 'easy' materials before embarking on fabrics that are more difficult to handle.

Yarns for machining fall into several categories. The finest yarn easily available for use in the needle is 50s machine embroidery cotton, which is also produced in size 30. The tiny reels are useful for small areas but otherwise are uneconomic, so it is better to purchase a 10g, or even larger, reel. All dressmaking sewing cottons have their uses as well as silk and man-made yarns, but it must be remembered that, in machine embroidery terms, 100 metres is a short length. Coton à broder, buttonhole twist and some lace and fine crochet yarns work well in the bobbin, as long as the operator remembers to work on the wrong side and follow the sewing machine instructions concerning slackening the top tension; this varies with the make of machine.

Thick yarns which can be applied by stitching through the middle or zigzagging over can be almost anything from rugweaving yarns, thick and very chunky knitting yarns, novelty threads both for knitting or weaving, Raffene, raffia – the list is enormous.

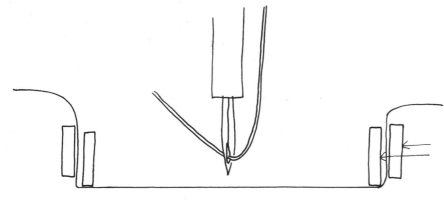

Cross section of fabric prepared for machine embroidery in a round frame. Note that the inner frame is slightly pushed through the outer frame to give greater contact with the bed of the machine.

fabric

frame shown
deep for diagrammatic
purposes.
The inner frame is
best bound with cotton
bandage so that it
grips to the fabric

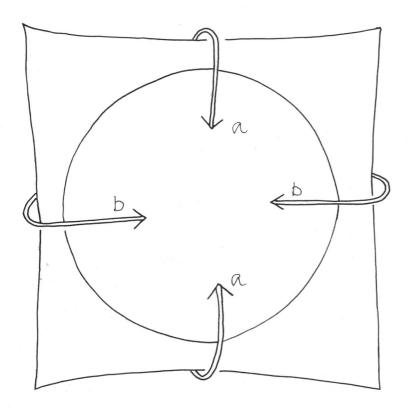

Diagram to show how to tighten the fabric in the frame to ensure that the grain stays straight. The edges a & a are pulled towards the centre, then b & b

Machine embroidery can be delicate, uniting with the fabric and creating a firm, washable, decorated surface. (It must be remembered that freehand work is impossible to unpick.) Amongst many possibilities for its use there are two ceremonial occasions for which this style of work is very well suited, namely weddings and christenings. The wedding veil could be embroidered with the initials of the bride and bridegroom, with the date, while the christening robe could have the baby's name worked on it and space left for future wearers – thus creating truly twentieth century heirlooms. Veil net is used for the wedding headwear but it could include applied areas in organdie or organza. A cotton or linen lawn would be suitable for the christening robe, or a polycotton fabric for the person who is concerned about the creasing problem of the natural fibre. As fine a fabric as possible should be obtained and further decoration can be achieved by doubling the material. A shaped hemline could be particularly interesting.

Machine embroidery is particularly useful for dress embroidery, especially for children, who grow out of clothes so quickly that the methods of decorating home-made clothes need to be quick too. Collars, pockets and hemlines can be decorated with patterns composed from the child's name; their full name, telephone number and address could also be added in an interesting way.

For the adult, a name on a silk shirt and other clothing adds the exclusive feel that is reflected in all the uses of lettering; and many of the man-made fibres lend themselves to the machined monogram. The design is very important and is similar to the considerations pertaining to whitework.

The equipment required for machine embroidery is, of course, a domestic sewing machine, preferably a swing-needle model, although much can be done on a straight-stitch type. For freehand work it is essential to be able to drop the feed dog or cover the teeth with a cover plate. The tensioning is then replaced by mounting the material in a shallow embroidery frame, carefully stretching the material in both directions. The correct needle size should be fitted to correspond with yarn size. Machine instruction books usually give help required for this. Spare empty bobbins are essential to save having to wind off after each colour. Should one colour only be used, such as white on a wedding veil, it is helpful to fill several bobbins at the start.

A pair of scissors with curved ends are another invaluable asset for cutting threads of the mounted work, as it is difficult to get close with straight ones; thread ends are cut, not fastened off, for most forms of machine embroidery, as it is unlikely to come undone.

In freehand work areas only should be marked out with tacking thread which matches the embroidery. As it is freehand a drawing of the work should be placed beside the machine and thus used as a guide; this is the skill of freehand embroidery. For other types of work, if the material is transparent, a heavy black line design can be traced through with a hard pencil.

Edgings for machine embroidery can consist of double hems which are satin stitched, strategically placed to enhance the final work. The edge can just be satin stitched or a scalloped edge can be worked with the machine. If the final effect is a single layer, two layers can be worked through and the backing layer cut away. Work on net can be mounted between two pieces of perspex and perhaps, if white, could have a thin coloured fabric placed behind.

Machine embroidery, whether freehand or worked with the foot in position, is generally small in scale and suitable for delicate-looking fabrics and precious items.

Machine Embroidery, Jennifer Gray, Batsford, 1973

14 Applique
and couching

Applique is a very early form of embroidery and felt applique has been found in Siberia dating from the fifth century BC. It appears in work of primitive and peasant cultures dating over many centuries to the present day. Little of the work of early centuries survives, perhaps because of its initial purpose; a very important use for applique in the mediaeval period was for horse trappings, flags, jupons and such ceremonial wear. These would not have been preserved except for some jupons which were placed above the tombs of warriors. Applique in this instance was a cheap substitute for encrusting embroidery.

Forms of inlay were used as wall hangings such as can be seen at Berkeley Castle, Gloucestershire, sometimes using leather, felt, velvet or silk. Pictorial scenes still hang in Hardwick Hall, Derbyshire, dating from the visit there of Mary, Queen of Scots.

The use of applique for quilts cannot be ignored and particularly those worked in the United States of America, the home of patchwork and applied fabrics, which has produced such beautiful pieces of work. Perhaps the reason for this was a question of economy, using up every scrap of fabric.

Work in the 1930s include pieces by Rebecca Crompton, who incorporated the use of a domestic straight-stitch machine into her work with applique and freehand stitches. Constance Howard portrayed the activities of the Women's Institutes in her panel for the Festival of Britain in 1951, the work being carried out by herself and her students.

At the present time much embroidery is worked in applique or uses applique as a major part of the background to other techniques. It helps to speed the work along and enables the worker to use many textures together without spending too much time on it. As fabrics are so exciting and varied, whether they be natural or man-made, it is nice to feel that so much can be shown in a decorative way.

The materials that can be used are unlimited. The range includes all types of furnishing and dress fabrics, leather, simulated leather, felt, acetate, sequins and sequin waste, beads, shells, mirror and many more.

The fabrics can be divided and sub-divided into groups: coarse, medium and fine; and of these, into ones which fray a lot, a little or not at all. If fabrics fray, the raw edges can be dealt with in different ways. A very coarse fabric that frays a lot cannot have the edges turned in nor can the edges be covered by a thin couching line. Perhaps such a fabric is not suitable at all! Other materials surrounding a very thick fabric could, perhaps, overlay the edges. Many fabrics can be backed by an iron-on interlining; these come woven and non-woven and in several weights. The edges will, of course, still have to be covered either with the appropriate thickness of couching thread or a stitch. Fine fabrics can usually have a very small hem turned in before stitching to the background. Transparent or translucent fabrics can create problems and the couching line would have to be employed again; interlining would be impossible as it would show. The zigzag machine stitch and straight stitch are invaluable even if they are eventually covered by hand, but they have to be done before mounting into a slate frame.

Background fabric to the whole work could, again, be almost anything. It

A panel for a child's room worked for an examination. Subject matter, the use of bright colours and the design make it a very suitable panel for a young person.

An embroidered panel, using patchwork techniques, for a calligrapher's workroom

helps to mount it on unbleached calico for additional support, particularly as the work is best achieved when on a frame. It is difficult to stitch pieces of fabric to others when they are all lying on a table, but possible when the background fabric is mounted into a frame.

A multitude of yarns are suitable and can include all those used for embroidery, weaving and knitting, as well as carpet and industrial weaving waste. Freehand stitches can be used liberally over the work. The machine can be used for decorating as well as assisting with the edges, and straight stitches can help by keeping layers of fabric together, as can running stitches or most of the other freehand stitches.

Letters should be stout and chunky as thin ones cannot easily be applied. Fabric can be applied, stitched round the edge, unwanted fabric cut away and the couching or a stitch used to neaten round the letter. Other applied letters would be used as a minor part of a piece of embroidery, particularly applique.

Applied letters are suitable for a quick method of labelling large fabric articles such as toy bags, bed and pram covers; also for placing initials or names on clothing, particularly for children.

Most couching methods are dealt with in the metal thread work section. Pure couching methods are very similar but the finished results can be vastly different because of the much wider range of yarns that can be used.

The scale of work can be much coarser than in metal thread work and the whole effect of background and applied areas resultingly much more dramatic. Couching works well with applique, the stitch often helping out by covering awkward edges.

All types of yarn from very coarse to very fine can be used and stitched down with matching yarn or one of a different colour. The couched thread can be pulled taut or can be bubbled, depending on the yarn and its purpose.

Amongst the ways in which lettering can be used, the two foremost are as an outline to capitals or as a continuous line for lower case letters. The capital can be highly decorated and the lower case have entwining motifs. This method is useful for children's panels or articles for their room and it is reasonably quick to do. Initials of parents, or the baby's name, can be worked around the frill of a cradle onto net, organdie or some similar lightweight translucent fabric; similarly, a pram or cot cover could feature the baby's name. In both these cases, if this is worked cleverly, the name or initial could be changed at a later date, or just another name or initial added or entwined. Couching is very suitable for applying letters to toys; for example, fabric bricks.

Applied fabrics in forms similar to letters, with the addition of french knots, rolled up felt and blackwork patterns

Creative Applique, Beryl Dean, Studio Vista, 1970

15 Metal thread

A flower form encrusted with various purls. Four heart shapes have been used to create a flower form, the hackneyed but still beautiful symbol of affection. This is a detail from a pincushion

A Valentine pincushion using silver thread and pins.

Metal thread embroidery is the rather loose term which applies to all forms of embroidery using a metallic looking thread. In the past silver-gilt added to the intrinsic value of the article or garment as well as enhancing the other methods of embroidery to which it was added.

Metal thread was worked on articles with blackwork patterns in Elizabethan times. The thread in this instance was made of drawn wire of silver or silver-gilt. This is contrary to the Chinese or Japanese work of many centuries which, up until recently, has been made from gold leaf. The gold leaf paper was cut into thin strips and wound round a silk core. The other main kind of metal working thread is a metal pigment sandwiched between plastic sheet.

The terminology for metal thread work is rather vague. It is shared with military and naval uniform 'scrambled egg' or 'gold lace'. There are specialist yarns sold in a limited number of shops and mail order establishments. There are other yarns made for knitting, crochet and pin pictures which can be used for embroidery. These can be purchased in knitting wool shops and haberdashery departments.

Articles decorated in metal thread embroidery are not practical and require careful handling. They can be costly if a large variety of different texture yarns is used for one article. It is also costly in terms of time as it can be a slow kind of work. There are ways to make a little thread go a long way and also take less time.

Because of its intrinsic value as well as its visual richness, metal thread is very suitable for commemorative work. It is something that can convey a very personal message which adds to its sentimental value.

The worker must be capable of very neat work. Accuracy when placing the needle from the right side and returning it from the wrong side is essential. The work must be precise; it can have a random appearance but this should be achieved with calculated positioning.

The choice of background material depends on its use. Metal threads work particularly well on a smooth or slub silk fabric or a good quality rayon imitation. Some woollen fabrics can make beautiful backgrounds, such as Welsh flannel, nun's veiling or felted materials similar to billiard cloth. With experience, the range of fabrics can be extended.

Most metal thread work consists of yarns laid onto the surface and tied down with silk thread. The surface is encrusted whilst the back of the work shows ends of the metal threads that have been taken down and hundreds of small silk stitches.

There are various methods of applying gold thread, the most extensively used being couching. This can be used for creating patterns by the bricking of one row to the next (see illustration).

The couched ends can be finished in three ways: they can be stitched and then cut close to the stitching, although this method is not always considered acceptable; they can be threaded separately and taken down with a chenille needle; or a hole can be made with a stiletto through which a loop of cotton can be passed from the wrong side, catching the end of the metal yarn and pulling it through. One or two threads can be taken down in this way. The choice of method depends on the background material, the metallic yarn and the position of the ends.

Fine gold yarns on reels are easy to obtain but have limited use. A good supplier will either lend or sell sample cards, which are very useful. Although these may be costly initially, they can be invaluable to the worker in many ways, from visualising the scale of yarns to calculating the ever-important final cost, and are especially useful to someone relying on mail order for supplies. A metre of very expensive cord may add great quality to other, cheaper thread, the resulting total being no more than having used all average-priced yarns. The sample card may help to make the wisest choice.

The yarn in the needle for couching down the metallic thread is most satisfactory if it is silk. A very fine thread called Maltese silk is traditionally used, but a thread easier to work with is dressmaking sewing silk, Gütermanns. It is made in several shades of gold and silver colour and it is a matter of preference as to which is used.

Yarn should be waxed by drawing it through beeswax three times. This strengthens it, helps prevent knotting and can also darken the thread. Size and

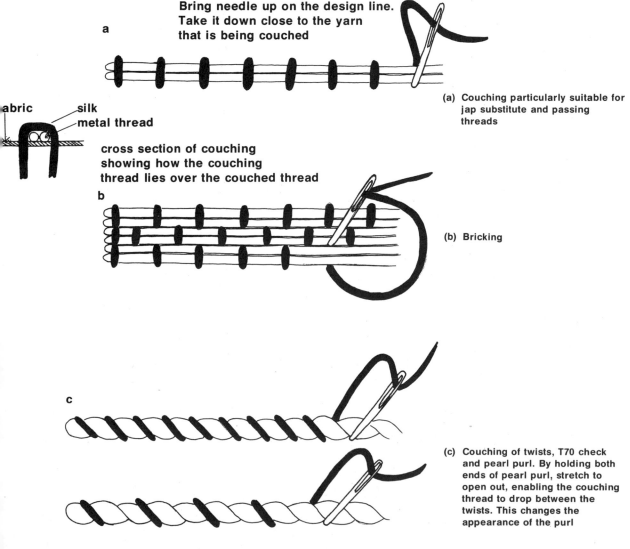

a Bring needle up on the design line. Take it down close to the yarn that is being couched

fabric   silk
metal thread

cross section of couching showing how the couching thread lies over the couched thread

b

c

(a) Couching particularly suitable for jap substitute and passing threads

(b) Bricking

(c) Couching of twists, T70 check and pearl purl. By holding both ends of pearl purl, stretch to open out, enabling the couching thread to drop between the twists. This changes the appearance of the purl

Bricking in metal thread, tying down with a thread that is suitable for couching. These diagrams show how the ends can be treated:

(a) taking down a lot of ends

(b) alternate ends; this is the least clumsy if the ends are taken down neatly

(c) the ends can bulge and do not easily line up straight

(d) there could be tension problems

Turning corners:

(a) one stitch for each thread at the corner

(b) two stitches over each thread at the corner. The second stitch has the effect of locking the first stitch, thereby making it easier to pull the yarn carefully but sharply to gain a good angle

(c) double thread over both couched threads, particularly suitable for fine thread

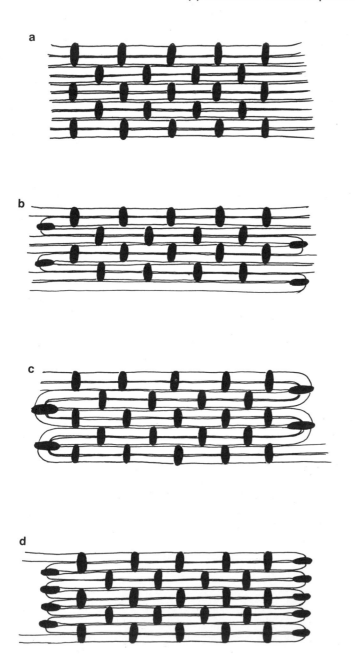

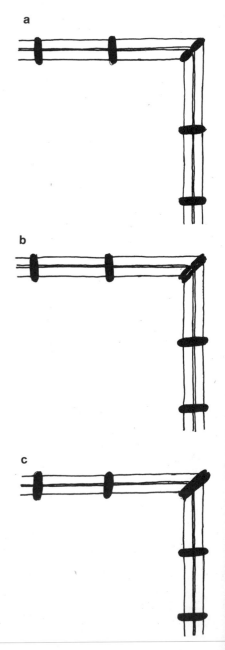

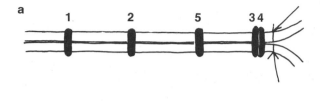

a

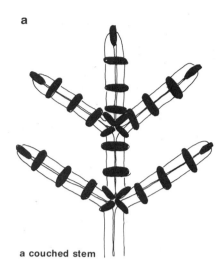

a

a couched stem

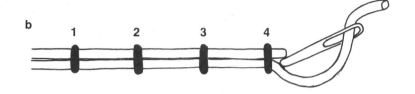

b

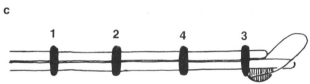

c

Taking down ends of couching:

(a) at arrow, cut ends of couched thread

(b) take down by threading into a chenille needle

(c) make a hole with stiletto. A loop of thread is slipped over metal thread which is pulled through to the wrong side.

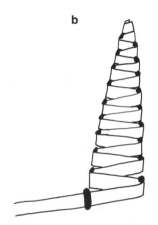

b

A method of stitching down plate

type of needle depends on the preference of the worker. The short between needle suits some people or the longer crewel needle aids threading with its long eye. A size 9 of either is quite suitable but no. 10 will be needed for the size 8 purls.

Illustrated in the photographs are several ways in which lettering can be embroidered with metal thread. The letters of REJOICE are directly traced from wood letters of 1900. These wood letters appealed so much to the author that there seemed no need to alter something that was very right. But the thoughts that were behind this word were due to the letters within the word. They work well together. Also, phonetically, the emphasis is on the 'J'; so this letter was more heavily embroidered than the rest. The 'J' became the focal point and the letters either side were less adorned. Several words were embroidered at this time and, with no thought of the church in mind, it seemed that words connected with religious services were very nice ones. The series of words was designed to brighten the home, with 'Home Sweet Home' as the centre piece; but this seemed foreign amongst 'hope', 'rejoice' and 'peace' (a lovely word).

An interesting way of treating metallic yarn and letters is to totally decorate the background but leave the letter void. This gives a great decorative quality to the finished work and is particularly suitable for box tops; it fits the shape of the box in a more satisfactory way and helps to incorporate awkward combinations of letters.

Full stops are great fun to do and can add a special quality, a raised stop giving quite a sensual feel to the work.

Infilling of circles, squares and other shapes. Always start from the outside and work inwards, as starting from the centre cannot guarantee the correct finished shape. When padding such areas, sew three layers for small shapes and more for larger ones. Cut the first felt pad to the finished size and reduce each successive pad by approximately 2mm ($\frac{1}{16}$in). Stitch down the *smallest* shape first, finishing with the largest on top and then treat as though it were background material

The intertwined initials of married couples make very memorable gifts for weddings and silver, ruby and gold anniversaries. These can be carried out and mounted as wall plaques or embroidered on decorative pin cushions, with the use of pins for additional messages. The pin cushion could also be wall-mounted.

A box lid or the inside of a jewel box could be embroidered with the recipient's name for an eighteenth or twenty-first birthday gift, or mounted under the glass top of a coffee table.

Metal Thread Embroidery, Barbara Dawson, Batsford, 1976

Types of Metallic Thread
traditional yarns or their substitutes

Jap substitute or Japanese thread. This is a wrapped yarn copying the Jap thread, which consisted of a silk core covered with a thin strip of gold leaf substitute beaten onto paper. It is sold on reels and comes in several sizes, called 1K, 2K, 3K, 4K, if gold, 1S and 2S, 3S, 4S for silver, 1K and 1S being the thickest in each case.

Passing thread is wrapped thread, this being wire wrapped around a central core.

T70 Twists (gold and silver) in several sizes. These are plied metal thread.

Check (gold and silver) again in several sizes, is a wrapped yarn with an apparent slight twist.

Imitation Jap (gold and silver) appears to be a cheaper metal. It can work in well with the threads which are made for knitting and pin pictures.

Cords are various and of different prices and thicknesses, some of which appear to have no name, or perhaps just a code number which varies from supplier to supplier. Cords can be made from the metallic knitting yarns and these can also be used for stitches as well as couching.

Plate is couched down and can be obtained in gold and silver.

Pearl purl is normally couched. This is a twisted wire rather like a spring which is pulled gently to extend its length and open it out so the couching threads fall between the twists. It comes in at least three sizes and a very fine one called X super or miniken.

Other **purls** are called **smooth, rough, check, bullion**. Their names depend on the shape of the rod that the drawn wire is wrapped round near the final stages of manufacture. Check, for instance, is a facetted yarn due to its having been wound around a three-sided rod.

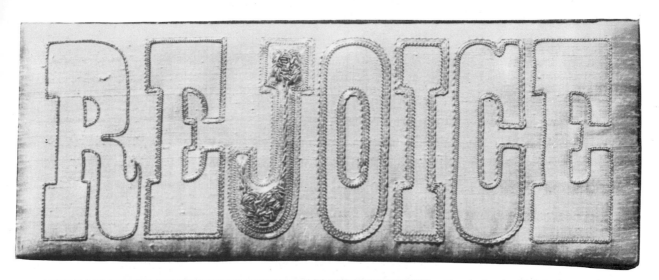

The design for 'Rejoice' was taken from printing wood blocks made in about 1900. Blocks such as these can be very useful to the embroiderer who lacks confidence in drawing ability but can line and texture an area competently. Various gold threads have been used here to embroider the word phonetically

The letter T worked by voiding the actual letter and turning the whole area into a formalized butterfly. Suitable for a box top, worked in silver metal threads

Letter D showing use of metal thread line and purl texture, worked in gold threads

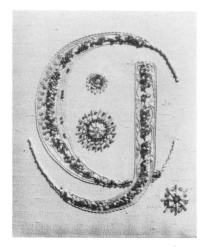

The centres of the C and J consist of rows of beads stitched diagonally across the gold cord

A monogram JRW worked after studying celtic letter forms. Metal threads are used to encrust this box lid

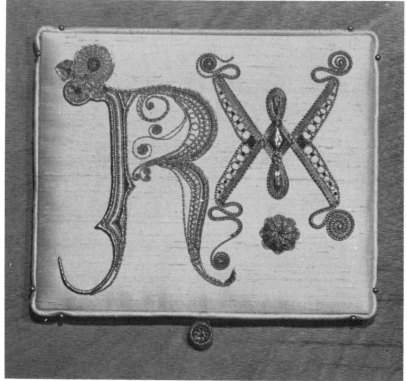

A box lid showing the initials MW using metal threads in a much less formal way than the previous monogram. French knots, beads and sequins are used in addition to the metal threads, purls and kid. The box is padded and contains a cushion filled with lavender, and is made to contain average size handkerchiefs

16 Ecclesiastical lettering
historic & modern

For hundreds of years letters have been used as decoration in Christian churches for three main reasons: as symbolism, as decoration (such as a quotation) and as labelling for the figure of a saint or apostle. The lettering has been used in a similar way in different mediums such as stone, wood and stained glass – not only for textile work.

The saints and apostles are frequently shown holding scrolls on which their names are inscribed. This is so in the period of Opus Anglicanum and its revival times. There are other ways of indicating a saint or apostle and this is by the symbol which he or she carries. Examples of this are a triple crown indicating a pope and the mitre, cope and crozier of a bishop. Symbolism is the literature of the illiterate, the vocabulary being large though not always consistent. Some apostles have several different motifs; for instance, Luke is represented by a book, a scroll or a winged bull. The amount of symbolism depends a great deal on the liturgy of the churches; Roman Catholics and 'High' protestant churches having much more symbolism and ceremony than 'Low' churches, while Reform churches and chapels are less well endowed with tradition and care little for these outward and visible signs.

Lettering on decorative borders is found on altar furnishings such as burse or veil, on altar frontals and as decoration on stoles, chasubles and copes. The lettering could be a quotation from the bible, a prayer or an acknowledgement to the donor or to the subject of the dedication of church or chapel – perhaps a regiment, a boy scout troup or women's organisation. In cathedrals where the public can casually walk through, this is a very worthwhile form of decoration, especially if it includes a quotation which helps the visitor to understand the aims of the people to whom the chapel is dedicated.

Another method of lettering which could be included under the heading of symbolism is the use of such letters as IHS. This is the acknowledged monogram of Jesus Christ. There are many learned explanations as to how these initials came to be, but perhaps it is better just to accept it as a very ancient sign representing something unknown but meaning much. ☧ or Chi Rho is another very ancient Christian symbol, older than IHS. Other symbols based on lettering include the Greek Alpha and Omega – the beginning and the end.

The fabrics suitable for wearing apparel or soft furnishing should be strong, dye fast and should drape beautifully. They should be lined or interlined wherever possible or appropriate. It is tempting to use dress fabrics but it must be remembered that the life expectancy of a dress fabric is much less than

The lettering around the edge of the altar frontal is basically constructed of three rows of couching. This creates a pattern from a distance which emerges as a message as the onlooker gets nearer

E and A worked for a chapel in Salisbury Cathedral. These letters include cords as they are on a large scale. The scale of work for 'REJOICE' would look spindly at this size

A very simple treatment of a burse using the symbols A and Ω in imitation kid

A mitre for the Bishop of Lewes, couched in gold on cloth of gold with layers of silk organza, based on the Chi-Ro and a cross

A mitre for Guildford cathedral with a padded Chi-Ro. It is interesting to compare two uses of this symbol by the same designer

This photograph shows the broken up area within the A. This is a hanging in Salisbury cathedral

furnishing fabric. In neither case is it possible for the layman to judge the rotting powers of the dyes used, nor whether a man-made fibre is affected by light – for example, white nylon can become yellow. Conditions under which many ecclesiastical vestments and furnishings are kept are not ideal and this should be considered when choosing background fabrics; it is disappointing when work looks shabby within ten years. Many churches do not suffer from too much light but can often be damp.

There are several things which need to be borne in mind if the embroiderer is working on a commission for a church. First of all, enquire of the incumbent and members of the congregation as to what they expect to be done. They may not approve of symbolism or lettering for liturgical reasons or because they do not understand the possibilities of the decorative quality of letters. Find out how closely they stick to liturgical colours, such as white and/or gold for feast days, purple for Advent and Lent and red for martyrs. The church may be adorned with blue all year round, which also represents the Virgin Mary.

An interesting treatment of the letters for ecclesiastical embroidery. The view from a distance is one of solid gold; from the middle distance the areas are broken up and a close-up shows interesting stitches. This is always a good way to think of large pieces of work and the embroidering of areas. When working a large piece of work in a small room, a simulated distance is achieved by looking at the work in a mirror

An economy measure when working a very large piece of embroidery in metal threads is to work part in padded gold kid and the rest in metal threads and purls. This also gives a very good contrast between ways in which the smooth kid catches the light and the textures show

When designing for an interior, one of the most important aspects is the style of design. The vestments and furnishings should blend with the style of architecture and decoration of the building, colour of the stone, tiles or brickwork.

The colour having been decided, the architecture and interior decoration of the building observed and the people who use the church consulted, the next consideration should be the technique, which includes applique both with hand stitches and using the sewing machine, metal thread work, freehand stitches or a combination of methods. Applique is a good method of decorating large areas with a minimum of work. But it must be remembered that these large areas of applied fabric should be held firmly to the background fabric to prevent sagging. It is economic in terms of working hours but the materials can be expensive. Many furnishing fabrics, if specially obtained, have a two-metre minimum order but the remnant counter often yields exciting bargains.

If a set of vestments and altar furnishings are being made to match, the question of scale of the design must be considered very carefully. A letter designed to be 5cm (2in) high can look interesting and in the right proportion but when enlarged to 15 or 20cm (6 or 8in) it can look rather dull. This sort of problem can be solved by dividing the letter into small areas, some decorated and some left plain.

There is no restriction as to the types of yarn that are used. These can be any suitable for the technique employed, from heavy carpet yarns and cords to machine embroidery cotton and metal threads, jewels and beads. Some sequins are gelatine or plastic that can disintegrate, so these should be avoided.

An amazing piece of work with applied canvas work dated 1956

Freehand stitches can be worked in large scale for the bigger hangings and on a tiny scale on the smaller articles.

Fair linen cloths and other linen articles are used in some churches. The main design can be modified for methods such as whitework, which needs to be employed where frequent washing is necessary.

The banner and wall covering are marvellous articles which lend themselves to embroidery. Their main function is decorative. A banner is sometimes carried in procession and for this reason the technique and fabric used should not be too heavy; also it should be remembered that the banner could suffer from the weather. The use of lettering for the banner is very obvious as it indicates whom or what the banner is representing. This can be written on both sides or perhaps just on the back.

The banner is not purely ecclesiastical; it has a long history and is used by trade unions and other secular organisations. The approach to design is similar to the ecclesiastical one although the sentiment may be different.

When designing lettering for wall hangings the main consideration is that it should be in proportion to the pictorial design and the overall size. The design should be bold and simple, as intricate complex stitchery is unlikely to be seen by most onlookers. It could be of bright colours.

Much of the colour in older churches has long since disappeared. It is often forgotten that mediaeval churches were elaborately painted; nowadays bare stone faces the congregation. With the new wave of interest in church decoration in this century, beginning with the flush of kneelers, it is exciting to realize that many churches are dependent on fabric of some kind for colour. Why not cover the walls with banner-like hangings to make the church visually warmer and more welcoming?

Kneelers are usually made in canvas work, as are cushions for stalls, but applique could also be used. Onlay and inlay methods would be particularly suitable for initials on cushions.

Kneeler designs have lots of different meanings in their lettering. Apart from the symbols already mentioned, there have been names of saints, local industries and industrial giants, the name of the town or village, local groups and so on. The difficulty of deciding upon subjects for kneelers is not the scarcity of inspiration but the very wide scope. It seems a pity that some resort to kits. Should an enthusiastic group of mothers in one church all decide to produce a pair of wedding kneelers, these do not need to be kept exclusively for weddings but can be used in a selected corner of the church. As always with such projects it helps to strengthen the ties with the church and makes it a living history of events within the area.

17 Designing for commemorative work

Special Royal occasions have always created a great upsurge in the production of commemorative articles. Some cheap, some expensive; some good, others of poor design; some were useful and others keepsakes or for passing on to grandchildren. For several hundred years any national occurrence affecting the lives of the people has brought forth some, or an abundance of, articles inscribed for the occasion with name, date and perhaps some pictorial evidence of the event: printed handkerchiefs on the launching of a ship; a mug showing the name, and wedding date, as a memento for a bridesmaid.

Embroidery lends itself admirably to recording an event. As the work is individually designed, it can be discussed by the embroiderer and the donor or recipient. There is great satisfaction for the person from whom the work is commissioned to be involved in an important event in somebody else's life and for the donor or recipient to help create a suitable object.

The word 'commemorate' breathes of memories not to be forgotten in rather a morbid way as it reminds one of memorials. Yet the Oxford dictionary mentions first that 'commemorate' means to 'celebrate' in speech or writing or by some ceremony. Mail order catalogues of mass-produced goods advertise wallets, thimbles, T-shirts, pillowcases and many other miscellaneous objects which can be personalised by the addition of name or initials. Perhaps there is a feeling of need for goods to be made especially for the individual customer or the mass produced article to have additional work on it to make it unique. It is interesting to note how many crowns and coronets were designed for embroidery in whitework in the mid-nineteenth century, as well as initials and monograms – the Victorian equivalent of the mail order catalogue, except that the work was given to the dressmaker or servant.

A pincushion in honour of a Queen, the design influenced by Queen Anne birth commemoration pincushions

Designing for commemorative work

Between the recessed florentine background and the kid name a light is positioned. An exciting idea as long as all fire precautions are observed!

'May and John' were created by marking the lettering design onto a piece of fabric which included a deep border. The spaces between the letters and border were cut away and fabric applied behind the spaces. This couching covered the raw edges of the letters and the border was padded

The full spectrum of embroidered articles can be exploited as commemorative objects. Dress and accessories are particularly suitable for certain occasions. The wedding veil could be embroidered by hand or machine with the name, initials, date and venue of the happy event; likewise a parasol cover for a summer wedding, ribbons for a prayer book or streamers for a hat or bouquet. The design could be fairly inconspicuous, yet there, to be treasured; or in a strong pattern that clearly shows. By careful design the pattern need not read as a bald statement but as a subtle decoration. Shadow work, net darning, needlepoint lace and machine embroidery are all methods suitable for fine delicate fabrics associated with weddings.

These methods are also suitable for garments for a new baby and christening clothes. The needlepoint lace is rather a slow method but perhaps something to occupy the new mother-to-be who has given up work and finds herself with unaccustomed free time.

Decorative embroideries commemorating events in one or more person's lives can take several forms – the inevitable embroidered picture, in relief or three dimensional work, springs to mind. Size can vary from miniature to a large hanging of wall-tapestry dimensions. Subject matter can be borrowed from the past, family trees, maps or poems, all illustrated in suitable methods and materials.

Birth is the time of satin and ribbons and traditionally a time for giving pins,

A pincushion recording the birth of a son. The photograph is held in position by a kid heart-shape which is stitched on the outside edge only. This edge is then decorated in purls and beads. The lettering is created by pins; lills are short but with the same size heads as longer pins

LOVE TO BABE] 13mm (½in)
TIMES REMEMBERED
TO YOU I GIVE Q
WITH AFFECTION
EXCEL TODAY PAT
ZOE JILL KATE

This alphabet gives good proportions of letters compared to the head size of the pins. Seven pins to upright of letter

No set of commemorative pincushions would be complete without one in memory of someone! Lavender taffeta silk background with black silk heart, ribbons and cog wheel sequins

particularly to a girl. In the past many articles of clothing were fastened with pins, therefore a pin cushion was a useful as well as a decorative gift. There is little modern use for a satin pincushion but it can be a very enriched gift, with no less use than a silver-plated rose bowl. It can be very easily constructed and requires no hanging. It is filled with silver sand (easily obtainable from shops specialising in aquaria) enclosed in a calico bag and then the pincushion made around it. The satin weave fabric, perhaps an oddment left over from the new mother's wedding dress, can be decorated in metal thread embroidery, couching or soutache work. The background fabric could also be fine linen with drawn patterns and satin stitch initials, backed with a coloured fabric to show through the withdrawn areas and add an interesting depth to the embroidery.

Family trees are exciting works to attempt. The scope of these is unlimited. Most techniques are suitable and size would be conditional on either the available space or the amount of information that it is desirable to record; this can include photos, easily attached with suede or kid. The format can be based on one of several recognized styles, such as the people represented by initials or names, and different branches of the family by different colours.

A club often has a committee table cloth or a banner. This can be decorated with the signatures, initials or names of members, which gives it a very personal nature as well as a record which can be added to over the years. It can be embroidered by one person or each member can embroider his or her own name. It can be made of one piece of cloth, or patchworked, or have names on a border which is added to the tablecloth. It can be in the club colours or monochrome or white. The signatures can be worked in chain, whipped chain or split stitch and headings or titles in raised chain band, a very versatile stitch for capital letters. The signatures or initials can be decorated with motifs applicable to the people.

Ruby wedding pincushion in Thailand silk, red leather heart using the wrong side of the leather for the second heart. The rest of the decoration is in beads, silver purls and pins

18 Designing for other things

The handbag or junk bag is a part of dress that can be decorated with name or initials either using a very sophisticated method in a classic style to last many years – perhaps metal thread work – or by applique and machine embroidery for a quick method styled in the latest mode, used, enjoyed and then thrown away. Little cost need be expended as scraps can be used or pieces of material from garments or curtains obtained at jumble sales. This also applies to laundry, toy and shoe bags, which can be named with contents or the person to whom they belong.

There are a number of soft furnishings which can be worked with initials; these include net and window curtains, cushions and bed covers. They are suitable areas for monograms or ciphers, names of friends or pets, or favourite story book characters. It is often easier to think of ideas for children's rooms, although this can be difficult to carry out as the subjects can become hackneyed, rather than decorative in an exciting way. There are many very well known cartoon-type characters already well documented in printed bed covers and pillowcases. But a complete alphabet can be personalised, the letters being used for favourite belongings or pets or making a special feature of the child's initial. A bed cover can last a number of years, longer than a cot or pram cover, so it is often a good idea to concentrate the energy of work into this. The teenager often has his or her own ideas, certainly enjoying lettering, perhaps not always applied to or where the parent approves! Many girls appreciate a quotation executed in a flowery method, and a sense of good taste can be encouraged in this way.

A pendant with an initial J in a heart shape created by french knots and bullion stitch. For comparison, the coin on the left is a new penny

One of a number of design sheets planning lettering decoration for children's clothes

A novelty use for lettering on a shoe worn by the Pope in 1888 when visiting Minorca

The usual methods of design, texture and colour need to be employed for these pieces of work, considering the fabric for its job and the type of embroidery suitable for the fabric. Considerations of washing should be high on the list for most soft furnishings, therefore care should be taken when choosing fabric from the ragbag.

Then there are articles which have little but decorative use: the pendant, the brooch, the necklace, showing name or initials. These are very rich if worked in metal thread work; a necklace rather like a collar could be exciting and ageless and therefore worn over a number of years.

For every day wear, pockets, collars and belts are amongst areas of dress that can be decorated. This applies to children's and adults' wear. It is difficult to show designs for dress as these need to be worked in the idiom of the fashion of the moment. Jeans were potentially a marvellous background to work upon but these must surely be coming to the end of their fashionable era; they have worked through the whole spectrum of use of clothing – working clothes, anti-fashion, fashion and decorated garments. But the replacement garment may well have room for initials on the pocket, the knee or the hemline. The anatomy of the body does not change; patches are always needed at strategic points. Imagine initial of the first name on one elbow and the surname on the other. The ideas have been exploited greatly by the badge brigade, patch manufacturers and screen printers, but there are still lots of possibilities.

Bearing in mind that many natural resources are becoming scarcer as time goes on, it is quite interesting to speculate on the way that dress may well develop in the future. Will the dowry system return, with young girls making or buying clothes which will last most of their lives? Will there be fashionless garments such as a cloak which will be expected to last much of a person's lifetime, coping with female figure changes, weather changes and suitability for times of day? In this case perhaps the name or initial could be applied to this article. Or will clothes be recycled instead of laundered, like the paper clothes of some years ago? Will people put up with dehumanising in this way and will they require to have articles of clothing which are tailored to them perhaps by the addition of their own cipher? Looking well into the future, one feels certain that, at least, everyone will continue to have his or her own name and this could be applied to clothing and fabric belongings, helping to retain personal identity in a world of identification numbers!

Handbook of Lettering for Stitches, Elsie Svennas, Van Nostrand Reinhold, 1973

NORTHAMPTON
MUSEUMS GALLERY FRIENDS OF
MUSEUMS AND ART GALLERY
HOWARD
1973
NORTHAMPTON

Detail from enormous panel in a
museum showing the donor of the
panel in lettering around the edge.
Here, the alphabet used is very
simple, reflecting the style of work
in the rest of the panel

Detail from another panel, exhibited
in a public place, commissioned to
celebrate 1000 years of English
Monarchy. This can be found in the
Pump Room, Bath

Little girl's outfit showing the
applique pocket 'abc'. An interesting
use of patterned and plain fabric

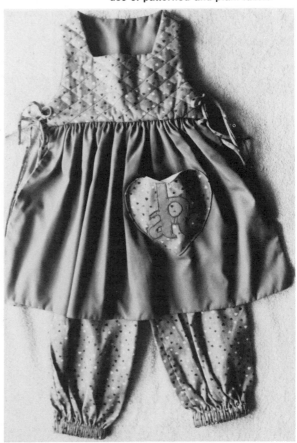

19 Designing for lettering

UPPER CASE
CAPITALS

decorative

lower case

INFORMATIVE

It is nice to make a rule. It is breaking rules that makes working with textiles interesting. Rules act as guidelines or beginnings.

The first ingredients of working letters in embroidery are a lot of enthusiasm and a determination to practise. A person's ability to enjoy manipulating letters is half-way to success. It cannot be a purposeless exercise, as letters communicate sounds, or are symbols, sometimes secretive, but they always carry a message for someone.

Throughout this book are many styles of lettering covering many centuries. In spite of current fashions, some forms of letters are more attractive to the onlooker than others, some letters are more suitable for a particular type of work, while some are more suitable for the occasion. At its simplest, take examples in letters applied to the seasons; these could be square and bare for winter, slimmer and lighter for spring, florid for summer and craggy in autumn. Yet, if the letters were to appear in a series of panels then a uniformity may need to be considered. Size or colour could help here, or perhaps a very simple lettering which could be filled in with different methods or stitches. But above all, the embroiderer must choose lettering to which he or she feels sympathy. The words to be used should be pleasant, hang well together and be enjoyable to both onlooker and worker. Combined, they should convey atmosphere or feeling appropriate to the embroidery.

In most forms of embroidery it is necessary to draw out the design. The lettering is achieved by some kind of drawing, whether pencil, paintbrush, scissors or sewing machine needle.

Letters are composed of vertical and horizontal lines, diagonals and curves, thicks and thins. It is very necessary to understand the composition of letterforms and each letter's relationship to the ones either side. So many words associated with the Christian church are nice, rich words. When embroidering a word it is not necessary to emphasise all the letters; one can perhaps treat the word phonetically, enhancing the stressed letter or letters.

The type of technique used should fit the situation, or situations can be created to fit the stitch. It is difficult to know when something like double-sided cross stitch would be a stunning success but perhaps someone will take up the challenge.

When using lettering it must be rememberd that the letters are created by arranging lines, areas, colour, textures and tones. The skeleton shape should be decorated with embellishment and ornamentation, respecting the character and modifying the appearance.

Gaelic lettering from Ireland. To increase your knowledge of lettering, collect drawings or photographs of place names, tombstones, public notices in different counties and countries. There are so many different styles of lettering, such as this observed in Southern Ireland. Do not forget the lower case place names always seen on major roads, an example of excellent letter design!

oceabpq

dg bead

ocean

Luyjwv

Lt xz hk

friends

Letters grouped in families using
very simple line and rounded shapes

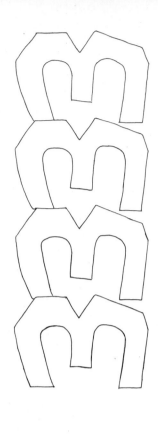

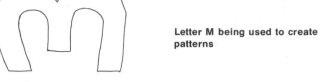

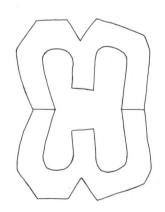

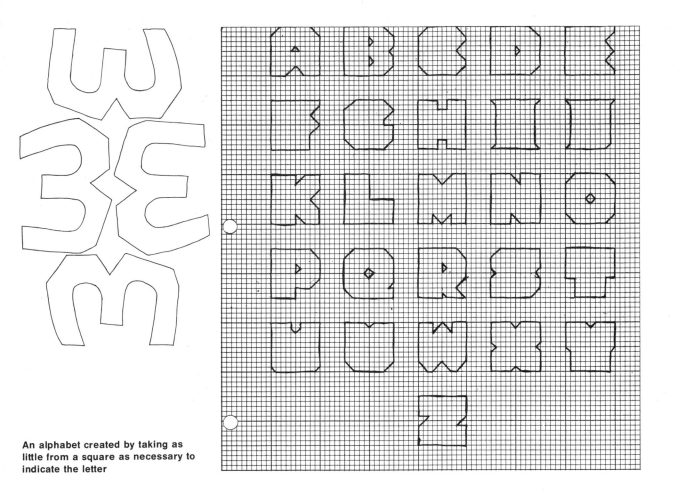

An alphabet created by taking as little from a square as necessary to indicate the letter

To achieve basic letter forms that do not depend on flourishing a writing implement, there are several exercises which are both enjoyable and instructive. A person spends a lot of time looking at letters, being bombarded by letters in shops, newspapers, television and packaging, as well as those that one chooses to look at. Letter forms are very familiar to all the sighted; it is difficult to create something new. But if the materials for lettering are different then the letter form is viewed from a different angle. For example, potato printing would have to be a mirror form of the letter. The letter form should be related to the shape of the potato. Cut the potato in half, notch the uncut side so that it is easier to hold and, with a sharp knife, cut away portions of the potato to create the letter. Brush on water-based paint – powder or poster paints are suitable – and print.

Another way of creating a letter form is to take a piece of card about 8cm (3in) square and cut away to form a letter, trying different letters in different card shapes, such as circles and rectangles. Try cutting away the maximum amount of card from a square to form a letter, or cutting away the minimum amount. Make a letter shape with lentils or pasta, or draw with a sand-filled cone with the tip cut off, onto a glue-covered card, leaving it to dry without shaking before getting rid of the surplus. Make a montage of letters cut from colour supplements, magazines, newspapers or other suitable publications. This encourages discrimination and helps sort out personal preferences. Try a border of cut up letters.

A monogram or cipher cannot be chosen, and some letters work together

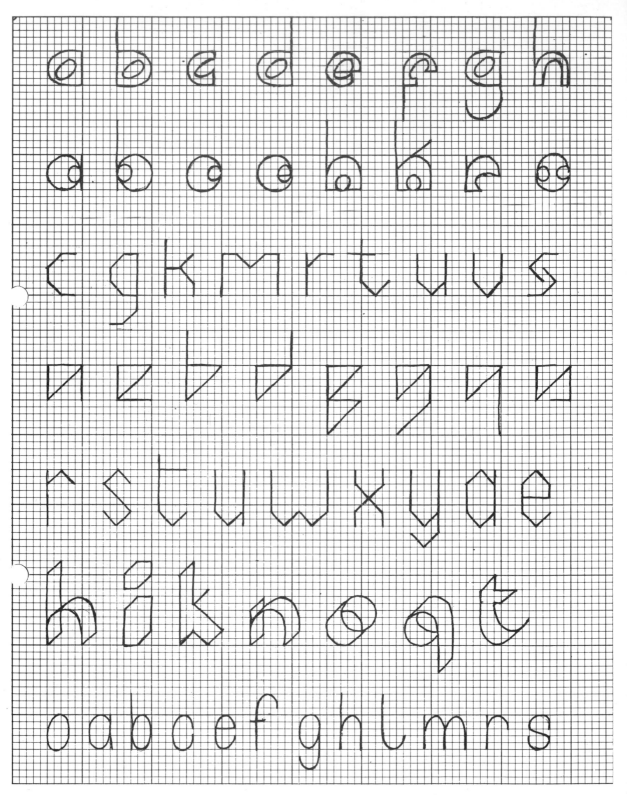

Experiments with letters

better than others. Additional decoration and a careful regard for good proportions help to achieve something satisfactory.

Some of the alphabets illustrated are not presented in alphabetical order but grouped in related shapes. A study of these should help the designer understand letter shapes and therefore act as a guide to adapting and inventing in a way suitable for the piece of work for which the lettering is required.

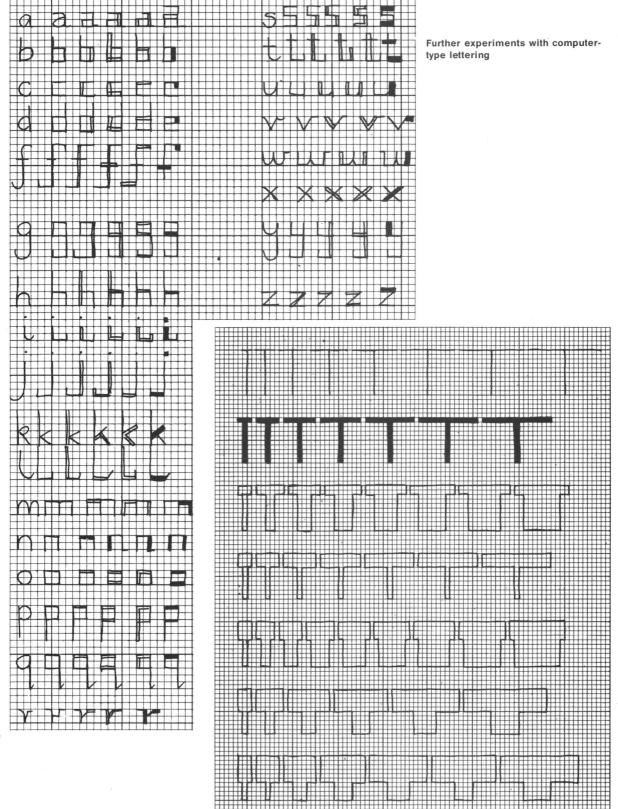

Further experiments with computer-type lettering

Experiments with the width of a letter

Snowdrops. This is a linear drawing taking the outside edges of leaf and flower shapes. The overlapping and falling nature of the leaves suggests a rounded movement. These round shapes could be used as a basis for letter O or C. They could be emphasised by the use of colour or gold thread on a motif

Index